RECYCLING BUILDINGS

RENOVATIONS, REMODELINGS, RESTORATIONS, AND REUSES

RECYCLING

BUILDINGS

RENOVATIONS, REMODELINGS, RESTORATIONS, AND REUSES

edited by

Elisabeth Kendall Thompson, FAIA

An Architectural Record Book

McGraw-Hill Book Company

New York   St. Louis   San Francisco   Auckland
Bogotá   Düsseldorf   Johannesburg
London   Madrid   Mexico   Montreal   New Delhi
Panama   Paris   São Paulo   Singapore
Sydney   Tokyo   Toronto

Architectural Record Books:

Hospitals, Clinics and Health Centers

Campus Planning and Design

Interior Spaces Designed by Architects

Houses Architects Design for Themselves

Techniques of Successful Practice, 2/e

Office Building Design, 2/e

Apartments, Townhouses and Condominiums,
2/e

Great Houses for View Sites, Beach Sites, Sites
in the Woods, Meadow Sites, Small Sites,
Sloping Sites, Steep Sites, and Flat Sites

Places for People: Hotels, Motels, Restaurants,
Bars, Clubs, Community Recreation
Facilities, Camps, Parks, Plazas,
Playgrounds

Recycling Buildings: Renovations,
Remodelings, Restorations, and Reuses

Architectural Record Series Books:

Ayers: Specifications for Architecture,
Engineering and Construction

Feldman: Building Design for Maintainability

Heery: Time, Cost, and Architecture

Hopf: Designer's Guide to OSHA

Library of Congress Cataloging in Publication Data
Main entry under title:

Recycling buildings.

   "An Architectural record book."
   Includes index.
   1. Buildings—Repair and reconstruction.
2. Architecture—Conservation and restoration.
I. Thompson, Elisabeth Kendall. II. Architectural
record.
TH3401.R4   721'.028   76-21329
ISBN 0-07-002335-2

The editors for this book were Jeremy Robinson and Hugh S. Donlan.
The designer was Elaine Golt Gongora. The production editor was
Patricia Mintz. It was set in Optima by University Graphics, Inc.

Contents

Preface

Call it renovation, rehabilitation, restoration, reuse or recycling: by whatever term it is known, the reclaiming of old buildings for adaptive or continuing use has become an important element in architectural practice and construction activity. Not only have the hard facts of late twentieth century economics given renovation a new feasibility, but they have pointed up the rewards — newly found desirable for esthetic, historic and humanistic reasons— which the character and space of old buildings offer.

Everyone benefits—including city governments, happy with the increased tax revenue—from the preservation, through renovation, rehabilitation or restoration of a worthy old building. When one revitalized building acts as a catalyst for other such projects in its vicinity, and a whole section of a city enjoys a renascence, the gain is not just in higher property values but in a return to values of a different sort, all but forgotten in the headlong rush to a progress in which bigness superseded the relationship to people, once a mark of our culture.

In undertaking a renovation project, a few guidelines are important to have, for pitfalls are always present in working with old buildings. For one thing, it is impossible, usually, to predict what conditions will be found once changes—structural or otherwise—are under way. For another, it is just good common sense to know as much as can be predetermined about the potential costs of rehabilitation and the possible investment return the building will make to the owner.

Basic to the financial feasibility of a renovation proposal is a use for the building which will be appropriate to its character, condition and location, and which will be profitable over a long period to its owners.

Any building under consideration for renovation needs close examination by experts in several fields: the architect, of course, whose skilled eye and keen imagination will see the possibilities—and the difficulties—in reusing the building; the real estate/marketing consultant who can advise on rental or sale potential; the structural engineer (and perhaps the foundation engineer as well), whose opinion on the structural condition of the building and on what is needed to bring it into conformity with code requirements, is invaluable; and the contractor, if the job is being done on a prenegotiated contract.

The importance of knowing the code requirements which will affect the job cannot be overestimated. Architect, engineer, and in some cases the contractor are fully aware (or should make themselves so) of the impact on the job that these constraints will have, but to the owner, (unless he knows from previous experience in renovation projects) the multitude of regulations governing what he wants to do will come as a rude surprise. Knowing what must be done to meet the law with regard to a particular use of a building is, therefore, both a basic consideration and a job for experts.

The extent to which a building needs changing to suit its future use is a decision the owner must make with the advice of his architect. Often the changes need not be extensive, and frequently it turns out that the less done, the more attractive the interior spaces can be. The exposed brick of an old wall, for instance, adds color, texture, and a sense of the original building which a new surface cannot give. On the other hand, there may be strong reasons for not exposing the old wall, and a new surface may be the most appropriate way of handling the design problem. In any case, the decisions of how much to change will determine the overall character of the finished building, and need, therefore, to be well thought through before any construction takes place.

Historic restoration is a different dimension of the rehabilitation process, often requiring a kind of detective work without obvious relation to architecture, engineering or construction, but vital to the exactitude of the restoration. This kind of restoration, though exacting, can also be exciting: the discovery of lost details, unsuspected color or decoration, secret economies (like the use of orange shellac over tin alloy leaf, instead of gold leaf, on the picture rail in Iolani Palace in Honolulu), make a romantic adventure of the apparent dustiness and mustiness of historic restoration.

To preface a book on new life for old buildings without mentioning the effect on us, the people, of preserving our heritage of architectural artifacts as well as our historic and architectural monuments is unthinkable. Such artifacts—the everyday buildings of everyday people—exist in every community, overlooked and unappreciated. Yet in their day, these buildings were not insignificant, either in purpose or in appearance. They functioned as bakeries, factories for foodstuffs as well as for merchandise, shops, offices—working buildings for working people. Today they are important to us to a degree that would surprise their original owners and builders: their scale, right for an era of smaller cities and fewer people, and their character, warm with the dignity of work, are once again qualities we seek in our cities. That the volume of space these old and still useful buildings offer is greater, in most instances, than can be afforded today is an added and very practical benefit of their preservation. The old building, whatever its original use, has superb attributes which were neither presumed for it nor desired from it even so recently as ten years ago.

For the investor with an adventurous spirit, with a concern for the quality and variety of the urban experience, with an eye for the scale and color of old buildings, and a sense of the human need for continuity from past to present and on to the future, renovating, rehabilitating or restoring the old building for reuse can be a rewarding and satisfying experience. This is especially true of the old building put back into use as a lively part of the daily lives of people. That is, in essence, the reason for this book, and the examples shown in its pages not only illustrate what has been done but suggest, it is hoped, further equally imaginative ways of giving new life to old buildings.

Elisabeth K. Thompson, FAIA

Renovation and Remodeling for Living

Happily, renovation of old buildings for use as residences is on the increase, for this gives life not only to the buildings themselves but also to the neighborhoods in which they stand. Some of these old buildings are significant—architectural monuments, in a sense, representatives of a particular period—and deserve on all counts to be preserved. But some are simple structures of humble use—barns, carriage houses, garages—relics of the everyday life of everyday people. These "architectural artifacts" are no less worthy, in their way, of preservation and indeed, they can and do restore a scale and character to a neighborhood which enhances the quality of living and increases the value of both the property itself and of its neighbors.

Given a new life in a commendably imaginative way, with just the right touch of sophistication for this period of time, and a great deal of sympathetic and thoughtful skill, such old buildings-turned-residences offer a special kind of delight to owners and guests alike, and to their neighbors as well.

Although the architect's primary work is particularly concerned with the design of new buildings, the old building ripe for conversion or for renovation is a challenge—and an opportunity with unpredictable rewards—which he can seldom resist. There is something about a barn, for instance, that is irresistibly appealing, a romantic atavism, perhaps, or the scale or volume of its space. The three barns in this chapter, like the stable and carriage house which are also included, show varying degrees of renovation, remodeling and preserved rusticity.

A trend of a different dimension is also evident in the selection of work for this chapter. A changing economy, changing customs, changing family conditions have brought to market buildings with the potential for reducing the size of dwelling units and increasing the shared amenities in ways not possible with the single family house. Here are two examples: a one-time hotel and a handsome mansion, refurbished and turned into condominium apartments of exceptional quality.

1

Balloon framing, an anonymous American invention of the early 19th century, has long been used for utilitarian buildings. Many older frame houses in small, older communities, are suitable for continuing usefulness. This house in the Hudson River community of Nyack is such a typical example. Built in the 1880s, it has now been remodeled to provide a residence and studio for a painter. All interior partitions were removed, and a new beam (two 2 by 12s bolted together) was put in on each level. Small columns were added at or near the two existing chimneys. Other changes included a new basement slab, new wiring, plumbing, and heating system. The exterior was largely unchanged. The basement level became studio, eating and cooking area. The front entrance, at the middle level, is adjacent to the unusual low-walled living room (opposite page, lower left) which overlooks the sitting area of the basement (below).

HOUSE AND STUDIO, Nyack, New York. Architect: *James R. Lamantia.* General contractor: *Kaplan Contracting Service.*

WEST ELEVATION

NORTH ELEVATION

Gil Amiaga photos

The old house was very simply converted at a cost of $16,000 into a comfortable, convenient and contemporary interior. The spacious living area and the ingenious opening of the living room to the rest of the house are notable features, as is the quality of each specific space.

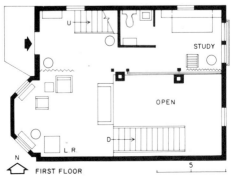

FIRST FLOOR

SECOND FLOOR

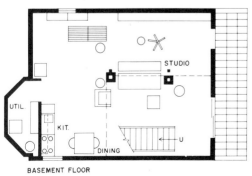

BASEMENT FLOOR

2

This 19th century stable on Boston's Beacon Hill, remodeled as a house, preserves a scale and character which is important in that historic district. But it also provides a place to live in town within walking distance of the owner's place of business, a relief from commuting, as he had been doing. In remodeling the old stable, some restrictions were imposed which determined the end result in unusually pleasant ways. The façade could not be changed because the building is in a designated historic district, and the side and rear walls precluded any new windows. The handsome courtyard was a natural and delightful solution to light and air for otherwise inside rooms. The rooms which surround the court are glass-walled, floor to ceiling, and the height of the principal rooms on the first floor was increased for added spaciousness and light.

TOWNHOUSE ON BEACON HILL, Boston, Massachusetts. Architects: *Childs Bertman Tseckares Associates, Inc.* Engineers: *Thomas Rona Associates* (structural); *Allan R. Morris* (mechanical/electrical). General contractor: *Scott McNeilly & Son.*

Hutchins Photography, Inc.

The courtyard is a tradition in the part of Boston where this house is located, and its use here proved compatible with the owners wishes. Its enclosed space acts as an additional room and is enlivened by a curtain and many plants. The court is the source of daylight for the principal rooms on both floors. In other parts of the house, colored clerestory windows, skylights and light shafts bring in natural light.

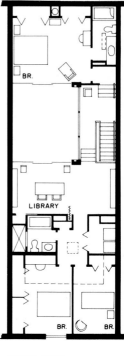

FIRST FLOOR

SECOND FLOOR

SECTION A-A

5

SECTION B-B

5

Jeremiah O. Bragstad photos

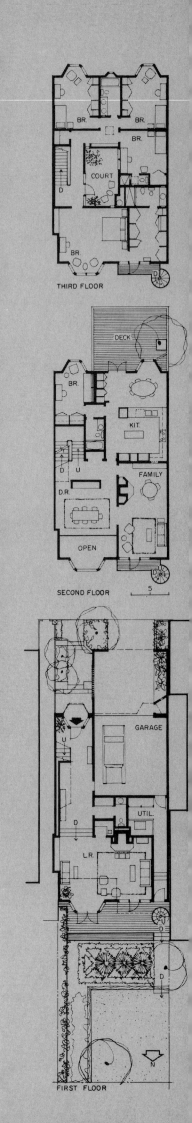

THIRD FLOOR

SECOND FLOOR

FIRST FLOOR

3 A two-story garage and ballroom structure adjacent to a large San Francisco house has been re-modeled and enlarged into a three-story urban residence.

Starting with two solidly-built clear span spaces, architect John Field has reworked the structure to allow addition of another floor and has opened the north elevation (above) to the dramatic views of San Francisco Bay. The large bay window, serving living room, dining room and master bedroom on respective floors, is echoed on the street facade by smaller bays (opposite above).

Great care was taken to relate interior spaces to each other, to the views and to the sun. Because the rear play yard seldom receives sun, a south-facing second floor deck above the driveway was added. On the third floor, a tiny open court catches sunlight for the interior bedroom. Cedar shingles tie old and new parts of the building together and the new house to the old one.

WALDMAN RESIDENCE Architect: *John Louis Field* of Bull Field Volkmann Stockwell partner-in-charge. Owners: *Mr. and Mrs. Murray Waldman.* Location: *San Francisco.* Engineers: *Pregnoff, Matheu, Kallam, Beebe* (structural), *O'Kelley & Schoenlank* (mechanical). Landscape architect: *Thomas D. Church.* Contractor: *Lester Lipinski.*

The kitchen-breakfast room, (above) and entry (left) face south, but the most dramatic space in the house faces north toward the Bay. The splendid two-story bay window (right) is part of the new construction added to permit four bedrooms on the top floor. The living room floor was lowered to grade (below) to allow maximum ceiling height and a new parquet floor installed.

Steve Rosenthal photos

4

At the high tide of Victorian beach resorts toward the end of the last century, the Rockingham Hotel in Portsmouth, New Hampshire, was cited in nearly every travel guide. Rebuilt after a disastrous fire in 1885 by Portsmouth brewer Frank Jones from plans by Boston architect Jabez Sears, the Rockingham's sumptuous rooms served several generations of tourists and played an important and continuing role in the city's economic life. Gradually, as rail travel declined and as standards of amenity changed, the Rockingham's future seemed less and less secure. It was recently purchased by the North American Development Corporation which commissioned Boston architects Stahl/Bennett, Inc. to convert the venerable hotel into condominium apartments.

The architect's plans recycle the original 87-room hotel into 35 apartments—mostly one-bedroom, but with some 1100-square-foot duplex designs as well. Where possible, significant interior details and material—patterned ceilings, marble floors, mahogany paneling, leaded glass windows, and original lighting fixtures—are being preserved, but all apartments will be renovated to contemporary standards of comfort, convenience and safety. New kitchen and bathrooms will be installed throughout.

A new wing has been added at the rear, along with new retail space, a pool deck, a dining terrace and other amenities. The old dining room has been retained and, after refurbishing, serves inside and outside trade.

The Rockingham has been built and rebuilt several times. On each of these previous occasions, parts of the old were preserved and new parts were added. The present architects understood this, knew their work was part of the same historical process, and enjoyed laminating a new layer of experience to these century-old walls. The care with which they have gone about their task suggests that this history may well continue and that future architects may find a good deal worth saving in the work just completed.

THE ROCKINGHAM CONDOMINIUMS, Portsmouth, New Hampshire. Owner: *North American Development Corporation*. Architects: *Stahl/Bennett, Inc.—Frederick A. Stahl, partner-in-charge: Allen Trousdale, project architect*. Engineers: *Weidemann, Brown, Inc.* (structural), *AMC Engineers* (mechanical); *Metcalf Engineering* (electrical); *Tsoumas Associates* (plumbing). Graphics: *Corporate Design Systems*. Contractor: *Noram Construction Company*.

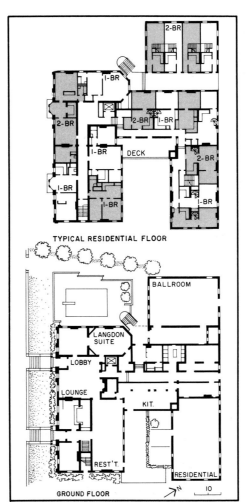

TYPICAL RESIDENTIAL FLOOR

GROUND FLOOR

The street level includes a restaurant and lounge as well as an outdoor cafe open during the summer months in the landscaped court shown in the rendering in middle of page

5

As an era of great estates vanishes, many communities are left with mansions too large for single-family occupancy. In the ordinary course of events, these old houses have been systematically destroyed while the estates on which they stand are subdivided. Except for the efforts of architect William Short, a similar fate would almost certainly have overtaken Guernsey Hall in Princeton. Built in 1849 to plans by John Notman, an architect who did a number of important buildings in Philadelphia and the Delaware Valley, Guernsey Hall came up for sale recently as a single-family residence in an R-1 district. The only offer came from a buyer who proposed to demolish the mansion, so Short—who was anxious to preserve it—joined his neighbors in opposing the potential buyer's petition for a variance. The petition defeated, Short organized financing, sold several apartments in advance, then went ahead with plans to convert the mansion into five condominium apartments.

The conversion, as the photos indicate, was carried out tastefully and with great concern for Notman's detail and decoration. Wherever possible, original materials were preserved intact. New materials were introduced sensitively, and the scale of generously portioned spaces was retained.

Because there was little precedent for this kind of project in Princeton, Short was not certain what the luxury, multi-family market would be. The apartments, as it turned out, sold in the $90-115,000 range without much delay and owners who committed themselves soon enough benefited by custom design features at very little additional cost. Included in the planning is a caretaker's apartment, maintained by the condominium—a feature that seemed mandatory but added considerably to the per-unit costs. The architect estimates that 8 to 10 apartments would be required to support a caretaker's unit feasibly.

Construction costs to the owners were about $350,000, a significant portion of which came from advance sale of the apartments. The remainder came from routine financing. The architect reports that from the beginning he expected to break even (or almost) and that is about how it has worked out.

GUERNSEY HALL, Princeton, New Jersey. Owner: *Guernsey Hall Inc.* Architect: *William Short (now Short and Ford).* Mechanical engineers: *Stratton, Farley.* Landscape consultant: *William Shellman.* Historical consultant: *Constance Greiff.* Contractor: *S. B. & H Builders, Inc.*

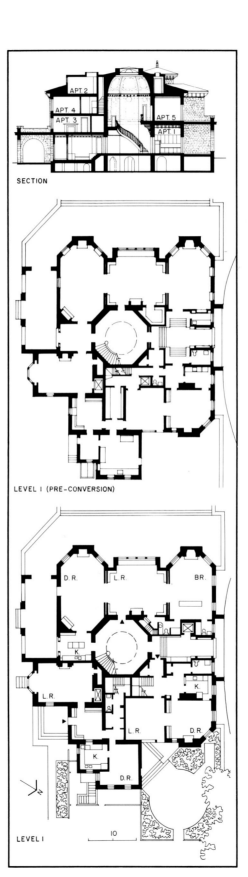

SECTION

LEVEL I (PRE-CONVERSION)

LEVEL I

6

When a client buys an old barn, he usually gets only a rough-hewn timber skeleton (right) on a stone foundation. The threshing floor, exterior siding and roof are usually in such poor repair as to provide at best only firewood. After the barn floor is removed, new levels, ramps and staircases are added to make the most of the interior volume. Early in the construction process, a new roof is installed and the timber skeleton is wrapped in new siding perforated by strategically placed windows and doors. A kitchen and bathrooms are added and the barn becomes a spatially complex house.

Architect Tigerman's clients chose a barn located on a large farm which they are turning into a natural game preserve. The family consists of four children from primary school to college age. The construction budget was quite low, but cannot be divulged at the client's request. The 30- by 60-foot barn had been burned out, but the whole foundation was there and its structure and knee braces were in good shape. A local carpenter was hired to put it all together again. He completely remade the exterior envelope, after which the electrical work was put in, exposing all conduit, switch plates and duplex receptacles, which were color-coded. The plumbing and ductwork are also exposed and color-coded. The silo foundation (top left) has been converted into what the architect calls a "womb room."

THE VOLLEN BARN, southern Wisconsin. Owners: *Mr. and Mrs. Harry Vollen.* Architects: *Stanley Tigerman & Associates; associates—Anthony Saifuku and John Haley.* Engineers: *Wallace & Migdal (mechanical and electrical).* Interior design consultants: *Stanley Tigerman & Associates.* General contractor: *Lee Whitmore.*

Philip Turner photos

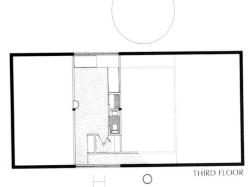

THIRD FLOOR

SECOND FLOOR

GROUND FLOOR

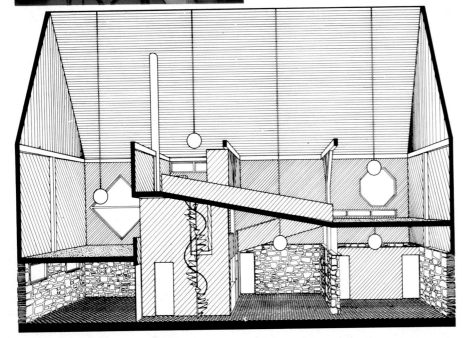

7

Take a gambrel roofed, Pennsylvania Dutch type barn, insert windows which make it smile like a Halloween pumpkin and wrap the whole thing in black asphalt shingles and what do you get? A form without precedent certainly, which some may consider a bit spooky. Others may feel it has a humorous presence rather like a figure in a Klee drawing. It is certain that the humble beasts which once inhabited this barn would never recognize their old home, but its present occupants—a veterinarian who is also an organist, his painter wife and their three children find that it suits them perfectly.

The plan includes a studio for the wife and accommodations for an organ. The scored plywood siding makes a handsome interior finish and provides a diaphragm structure which stiffens the 100-year-old barn. All conduit, heating ducts and plumbing are exposed and color-coded blue, red and yellow respectively. All glazing is gray-tinted plate. Costs were quite low, but the client does not wish to reveal them.

FROG HOLLOW, southern Michigan. Owners: *Dr. and Mrs. James Christiansen.* Architects: *Stanley Tigerman & Associates; associates—Anthony Saifuku and John Haley.* Engineers: *Raymond B. Beebe & Associates* (structural); *Wallace & Migdal* (mechanical and electrical). Interior design consultant: *Stanley Tigerman & Associates.* General contractor: *Lester & David Krumerie.* Principal subcontractors: *F. H. Klugh & Son* (mechanical); *Mead & White Electric* (electrical); *Ace Plumbing Co.* (plumbing).

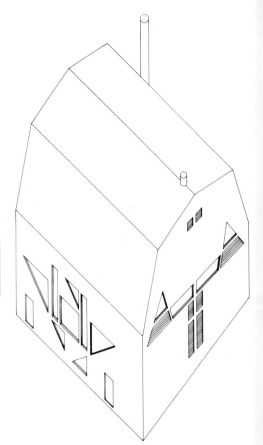

Philip Turner photos

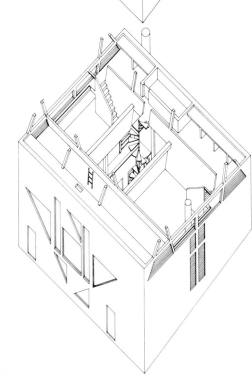

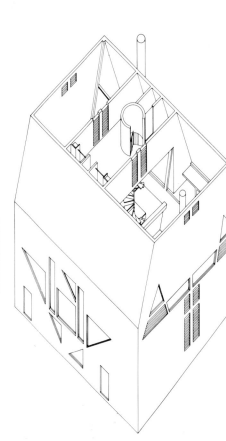

8

Old Connecticut barns are much sought for renovation, as was this one in Greenwich. The existing wood frame sits on a masonry base and is sited so that entrances occur at both ends but at different levels. As replanned by the architects, the lower level, which opens to the rear of the property, is given over to childrens' bedrooms, guest bedroom, storage and recreation. The upper levels, containing living and dining spaces, kitchen, balconied master bedroom and studio, are oriented toward the front. The wooden superstructure offered opportunities for loft-like planning—opportunities the architects exploited vigorously as the photographs indicate. To tie the levels together and provide a single but powerful point of reference, the architects employed a huge photomural (photos, opposite page) with an old railroading subject.

While much of the original structure and some of the barn-like spatial volumes remain, no real attempt has been made to continue the rustic theme with the new work. Indeed, the interior almost totally denies the origin of the structure. The additions and changes which give it so contemporary a character have been made with unusually high standards as evidenced by the materials, detailing and finish used.

BARN RENOVATION, Greenwich, Connecticut. Architects: *Gwathmey-Siegel.* Contractor: *A. LoVito, Inc.*

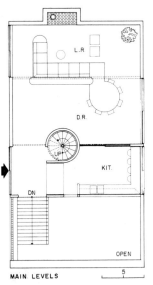

MAIN LEVELS

LOWER LEVEL

David Franzen photos

SECTION
5

9 Built just after the turn of the century, this carriage house was renovated for $85,000, a figure much less than the $250,000 that would be required, according to the architect, to build a similarly sized house today. The 100- by 40-foot house contains 7000 square feet, so on a cost per square foot basis, the remodeling is reasonably priced.

When purchased by the owners, the concrete block building was as it had always been—unfinished garage space. Architect Myron Goldfinger made minimal changes to the entrance façade (above, left), retaining the small 6-over-6 windows, and complementing the austere but mellow block walls with a simple, broad slab leading to the door. However, the large dormer

roofed over in plastic suggests the light, contemporary interior (above photo, right) beyond.

Inside, the architect has opened the living space to a bedroom loft above, and to the outdoors by replacing old windows with three sliding glass doors. The cutaway section of the second floor permits a second-story dormer to light both floors, while affording a first-floor view of exposed timber trusses and tension rods.

The conversation area, formed by 9-foot-long built-in banquettes, achieves more height by being sunken. Conforming to the opening above, the banquettes provide an obvious separation of spaces, as well as storage.

The openness of the plan extends to the kitchen and pantry, separated from the dining area by a fireplace and two low counters with butcherblock tops. Lounging pillows on the floor in front of the fire pleasantly contrast—as do the exposed timbers—with the hard finishes generally used in the formal living and dining areas.

The first-floor gallery (see plan, page 20) retains the original brick floor, and wood and brass stalls of the former stable; the space is now used by the owners as a pottery studio.

PRIVATE RESIDENCE, Bedford, New York. Architect: *Myron Goldfinger*. General contractor: *John Allen*.

10

This small basement apartment in New York City was remodelled by Paul Rudolph for psychotherapist Joanna Steichen, whose distinguished art collection includes photographs by her late husband Edward Steichen. (Rudolph was the architect for the famous "The Family of Man" photographic exhibition created by Edward Steichen for the Museum of Modern Art in 1955.) Rudolph insists that his own contribution to the design of Mrs. Steichen's apartment was modest: "She is a friend, the remodeling was down the street from where I live. I just gave her practical advice, produced a few working drawings and dropped in from time to time to see how things were coming along." In other words, he helped her create a setting for herself, her work and her collection, but did not do it for her.

They started with a basement apartment with huge windows facing south and east. It has an 18 ft-6 in. high major space and a two-story area with heights of 8 ft-6 in. per story. Two new levels were added to the high space—a mezzanine which doubles as a sleeping loft for guests or a sitting area (opposite page, middle) and, a few steps above it, a bridge which serves as Mrs. Steichen's study and work area (opposite page, bottom left). The new levels are supported by light steel members bearing on existing masonry. Below the sleeping loft is a low-ceilinged, intimate seating alcove (opposite page, top and bottom right), ideal for parties or group therapy. The dining area is located under the work study bridge and the high-ceilinged space which remains is part of the living area. Wall finishes, lighting, cabinet work and shelving have been carefully detailed to enhance the art collection. The cove lighting above the seating area consists of 7-watt bulbs 1 ft on centers.

APARTMENT RENOVATION, New York, New York. Owner: *Joanna T. Steichen*. Architect: *Paul Rudolph; project architect—Peter Mullen*. General contractor: *The Ormar Building Corporation*.

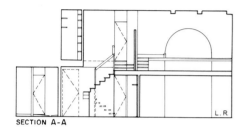

SECTION A-A

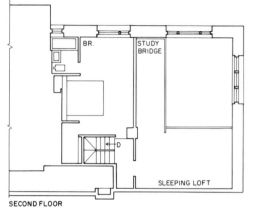

BR. STUDY BRIDGE

SLEEPING LOFT

SECOND FLOOR

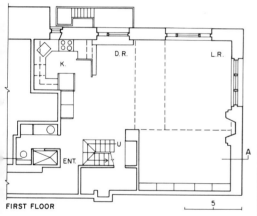

K. D.R. L.R.

ENT.

A

FIRST FLOOR 5

Mrs. Steichen's collection consists in part of small objects, for which Rudolph has designed appropriately scaled shelving. A few large objects occupy the high-ceilinged space. All the new walls are metal stud and drywall. To conceal the difference between the old walls and the new walls, a spray-on textured acoustic surface was applied to all the walls and painted with a flat oil base paint. The ceilings are white and so are most walls. Where Edward Steichen's photographs are assembled, however, a dark brown has been provided and is unusually effective.

Cervin Robinson photos

Renovation
and Remodeling
for Business

The warehouse, loft and factory buildings of a bygone day, abandoned when a changing technology or a shift in the location of a city's commercial-industrial district made them obsolete, have begun to have new and useful lives, converted with skill and imagination—and economy—into interesting and unusual places to work. Since such buildings are frequently found in clusters in one section of a city, the renovation of one often leads to the revitalization of a whole area, with a consequent benefit in property value increase.

The clear-span loft space of this kind of old building makes it eminently suitable for remodeling and redesign to meet the need of almost any kind of business, sometimes in fairly traditional ways, sometimes in highly innovative form, as for the advertising offices of Dancer–Fitzgerald–Sample in San Francisco. The openness of loft space gives almost as much design freedom as a new building does, once the requirements have been met for bringing the old building up to code in structural, electrical and mechanical systems. The offices for the old *Saturday Review* magazine are a case in point: the brick walls of the building could not alone meet San Francisco's lateral force code, and so a steel frame was erected inside the building to provide the necessary reinforcement. The interior was then opened up with an unusual interplay of levels.

The economic advantage of renovating an old building has gained importance as the economics of new building have escalated. One of the significant examples of the value of finding a feasible new use for and renovating an existing, sound building is the old City Hall in Boston, where relatively slight changes netted a sizeable increase in usable space and brought the building up to modern standards of circulation, lighting, and air conditioning.

Architects are often the first to discover the possibilities of an old building, and for a long time have been proud to locate their offices in them. One of the most unusual such offices is the old Feather Factory, literally a building in which feathers were prepared for commercial use. Equally pleasant, but of a different scale, are architects' offices in old houses, carriage houses, lofts and warehouses. Included in this chapter are examples of all of these, along with the types mentioned above for office and industrial use.

1

Over a hundred years before the Boston City Hall Competition of 1962, another competition for a Boston city hall was held. The winning entry of that one, designed by Gridley J. F. Bryant and Arthur Gilman, was as influential in its time as its worthy successor. The style was known as Second Empire and the architects of many public buildings around the United States drew inspiration from the Boston building, completed in 1865 at a cost of about $500,000.

When the new city hall was occupied late in 1968, the Boston Redevelopment Authority sought a private developer who would respect the architectural character of the building while converting it into a prestigious office building with commercial and restaurant facilities. Architectural Heritage Inc., a nonprofit corporation, was interested in seeing the building properly renovated. It sponsored, in 1969, preparation of a historical report which underlined the BRA's concern for preservation of the existing structure and demonstrated the economic feasibility of the project. Based upon that report, a subsidiary of Architectural Heritage, Old City Hall Landmark Corporation, and Graham Gund, at the time an urban design student at the Harvard Graduate School of Design who had been part of the project from its inception, were named co-developers. They in turn chose Anderson Notter as architects.

Today, almost all of the 80,000 square feet of renovated office and commercial space in the rehabilitated granite building has been rented. The original central staircase, and two ancient elevators added soon after the building was finished, occupied a large hall surrounded by interior bearing walls, upper plan, right. That space was large enough to accommodate a new core with two separate egress stairs, two modern elevators, toilets and circulation corridors for the entire floor. Thus, the perimeter, as in a standard contemporary office building, was left entirely free for development of office and secretarial space. All windows have been re-glazed with single sheets of glass (left), the only visible exterior change, but one which strengthens the original design.

The two lower floors of the old city hall have had substantial interior revision as well. A new entrance passage (bottom left) leads through an arched glass door that contrasts elegantly with the clustered stone columns. The original dedication plaque is visible above the elevators. The right half of the main floor has been occupied by the First National Bank of Boston (right bottom), another interior by the architects. The other space on the left half of the main floor is suitable for use as a restaurant with spacious dining rooms. In addition, a group of smaller dining rooms, bar and kitchen is located in the basement and serves both the public and the building's tenants. An outdoor dining patio just off the bar, provides for pleasant summer luncheons.

OLD CITY HALL, Boston, Massachusetts. Owner: *Old City Hall Landmark Corporation*. Architects: *Anderson Notter Associates Inc*. Engineers: *LeMessurier Associates Inc*. (structural); *Progressive Consulting Engineers, Inc.* (mechanical); *Herosy Associates, Inc.* (electrical). General contractor: *Kirkland Construction Company*.

Jon Maguire photos

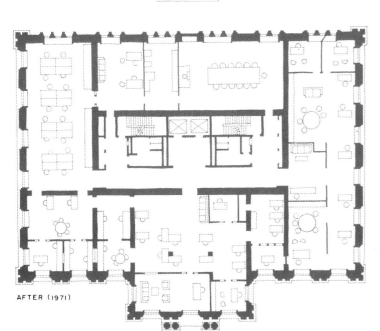

BEFORE (1865)

AFTER (1971)

The most successful office floor interior completed to date, and the only one by the architects, Anderson Notter, is occupied by the Massachusetts Housing Finance Authority, a quasi-public agency which lends money for construction of low- and moderate-income housing. Its spaces (photographs below and bottom plan) express most clearly the architect's intent to carry the theme of the building's arched windows by creating new arches faced with natural-finish wood in interior partitions. These arches, sometimes glazed, form a strong axis that seems entirely appropriate in a classical building.

The dummy window (above) has a painted cat on its sill. Yang's apartment has been designed primarily for entertaining and the contemplation of art. Books, records and miscellany are concealed in extensive cabinet work, and surfaces are kept clear. His office (not shown) is on a lower floor.

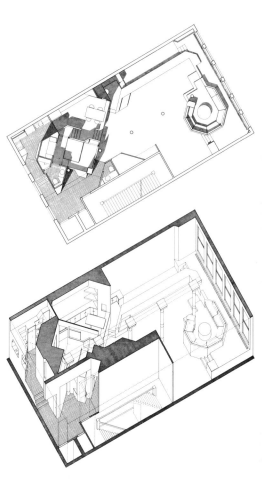

2

New York City's Soho district is the place to go to admire its cast iron fronts and to look at paintings in its burgeoning art galleries. On their way down Prince Street, however, some art lovers may miss a remarkable *trompe-l'oeil*—a mural of a cast iron front at right angles to a genuine cast iron front. This witty deception was instigated by architect Hanford Yang (who owns the landmark building), the New York City Landmarks Commission, City Walls Inc. (which has promoted other murals on the exterior walls of old buildings), and the National Endowment for the Arts (which provided the money). The mural was designed by Richard Haas, a photorealist painter for whom

cast iron buildings are a frequent subject. He made a carefully dimensioned drawing which was scaled up, transferred to the wall and filled in by professional sign painters.

The real cast iron front is one of the loveliest in New York. It is one of the few that is not criss-crossed by a fire escape, so the proportions can be clearly seen. As the photographs (opposite page) indicate, the floor heights decrease by 18 inches each as they go up, an optical device to make the building look taller. Architect Yang bought the building for its looks and set about transforming it into an office and home for himself.

It had once been a toy factory with tin

ceilings, and was in very bad repair when Yang acquired it. After making basic repairs and installing a new mechanical system, Yang began to experiment with the interior spaces. His workmen were local artists who were willing to change the heights, sizes and positions of the various design elements, as Yang tested them. Much attention was paid to the placement of his art objects. As can be seen in the photograph above, all the cast iron columns are exposed. The partitions have been cut and turned to accommodate them. Walls are white, the carpets are grey and the natural wood surfaces have a high-gloss finish. The only color is provided by the art.

Along with a number of other groups in San Francisco, when Dancer-Fitzgerald-Sample, Inc. decided to find new office space in 1968, they took a close look at the old warehouses along the then drowsy north waterfront. When the architects told DFS that the tentatively selected 1907 structure was sound, DFS plunged into the remodeling with the vigor that only an advertising agency could muster. Selecting a building committee with representatives from all the departments, including the secretaries, they began to study the problem. Even though they admit in retrospect that the architect's recommendations were always the best ones in the end, the committee analyzed everything from building procedures to fabric and color choices. Two principal design problems had to be solved; first, the arrangement of necessary work spaces on the second floor which, at the same time, would preserve everyone's view of the existing timber trusses; and second, an entrance and main stairway that would draw visitors to the second floor from the street with as little effort and much drama. The photographs seen above right and the photos following show how handsomely the criteria were met. Starting with straightforward loft space (below left) the client and architect placed most of the private offices around the perimeter. All are roofless so that the structure can be seen above. The inviting entrance, (left) visible through the arched façade from the street, focuses on a reception desk that is halfway to the second floor. Views up into the vaulted space from that point, (opposite), tie parts of the design together.

DANCER-FITZGERALD-SAMPLE OFFICES, San Francisco, California. Architects: *Hugh Stubbins/Rex Allen Partnership—R. A. Zambrano, Gwin Richards,* project architects. Engineers: *Geoffrey Barrett* (structural); *O'Kelly & Schoenlank* (mechanical); *Mel Cammissa* (electrical). Contractor: *Robert L. Wilson, Inc.*

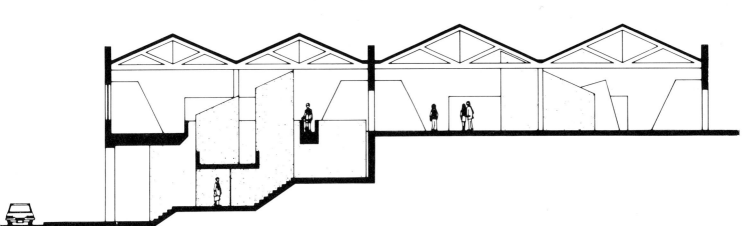

Sloping-walled offices, above, are open to the trussed space but have curtains for visual privacy. The bridge (right) connects a glass-walled conference room with the offices.

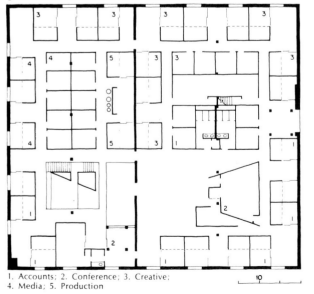

1. Accounts; 2. Conference; 3. Creative;
4. Media; 5. Production

Harris and Davis photos

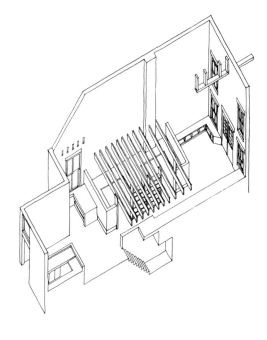

4

This young firm took on as its first project the remodeling of an 840-square-foot space for its own office. The space is on the third floor of a nineteenth-century commercial loft building, and originally it had two levels. The architects put new joists into the existing joist pockets to create the feeling of separation between the reception area (photo top right) and the rest of the office (photo above). Below the new joists are individual work stations for each of the firm's four partners, and above—in due course—there will be a mezzanine for expansion. The conference area (photo above right) is the only part of the office where the full 19-foot height of the loft space is unobstructed; it stands at the opposite end of the office from the raft of colored banners that are the office's other memorable feature.

OFFICE FOR BAKER ROTHSCHILD HORN BLYTH, Philadelphia, Pennsylvania. Architects and general contractor: *Baker Rothschild Horn Blyth.*

5

This trim rehabilitation of a sound old loft building to expand the adjoining offices of a non-profit foreign student exchange organization represents a sensitive, economical example of urban renewal. The architectural endeavor was to restore the straightforward factory aspect of the 1880's building by exposing the timber joists and brick bearing walls, and by making all necessary alterations to the exterior conform in scale and detail to the original. On the interiors, all exposed surfaces are painted off-white with bright splashes of color in built-in niches used for bookshelves and file cabinets. All these are bathed with incandescent light. Floors are carpet, except for quarry tile in the entrance lobby and in wash rooms. Special carrels were designed for use as individual work stations to provide some acoustical and visual privacy without resorting to completely enclosed offices. The result is a very fresh, congenial ambience created at low cost.

OFFICES FOR THE AMERICAN FIELD SERVICE, New York City. Architects: *Harold Roth—Edward Saab.* Engineers: *Associated Engineering* (structural); *John L. Alfieri* (mechanical and electrical). Lighting consultant: *Sylvan R. Shemitz.* Contractor: *Raberg, Nusser and Raberg.*

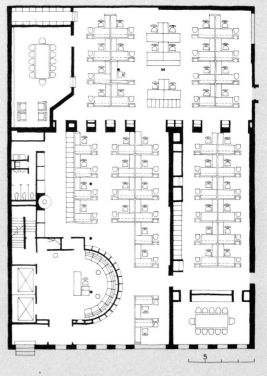

Robert Perron photos

6

Its builders named it "La Puerta del Sol." Constructed in 1925 at the height of Florida's land boom, the picturesque structure (below) was the hinge in millionaire-developer George Merrick's dream for Coral Gables. Merrick envisioned the arched opening as the gateway to the city, and the surrounding complex of towers and terraces, colonnades and winding stairs as a high-style residential and cultural community. Only the great arch was built. The Depression splintered the rest of Merrick's dream. During the lean years of the 30s, the apartments were abandoned one by one. Pigeons claimed the clock tower. Three decades of quietude followed as the stream of Coral Gables life flowed elsewhere.

In the late 1960s, a corporation was hurriedly formed to buy the arch (now called Douglas Entrance) because it had fallen to real estate interests whose intention was to demolish it to make way for a supermarket. When the corporation appeared unable to save the structure, the architectural firm of Ferendino/Grafton/Pancoast purchased the property independently and began converting it for their own use.

Ferendino/Grafton/Pancoast, it should be said, were most assuredly conscious that in acquiring the Douglas Entrance they were preserving an important Coral Gables landmark. But they ventured into the project only after satisfying themselves that it represented a sound financial investment. Thanks to depreciation, and in spite of extensive restoration and landscaping, long-term costs will be appreciably less than for comparable new space. Whatever efficiency is lost to sprawl is more than compensated by the richness and variety of architectural ornament and spatial experience.

OFFICE OF FERENDINO/GRAFTON/PANCOAST, Coral Gables, Florida. Architects and engineers: *Ferendino/Grafton/Pancoast.*

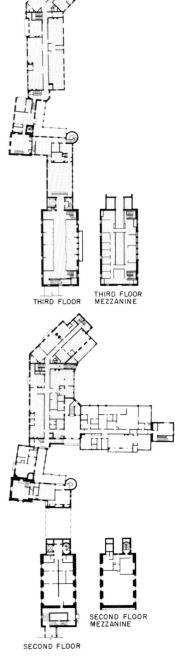

THIRD FLOOR

THIRD FLOOR MEZZANINE

SECOND FLOOR MEZZANINE

SECOND FLOOR

Joseph W. Molitor photos

The great double-height ballroom (above) has become office space for the firm's principals. Tucked under the splendid ornamental ceiling, a mezzanine houses accounting and administrative functions. Across the elevator lobby, in the space over the arch, the architects have installed an audio-visual center for client presentations. Drafting and design teams are grouped in several of the old apartments reached by a third-floor colonnade and the firm's engineers occupy space on the building's first and second floor. Both Grafton and Ferendino sold their homes to take apartments in the structure. Grafton's apartment (left) looks out over landscaped court.

Much of the first- and second-floor space outside the tower is now rented to professional tenants who form, with the architects, a sympathetic community.

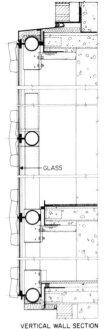

Balthazar Korab

VERTICAL WALL SECTION

The original loft building (below) was stripped to its concrete frame and sheathed in an almost-all-glass curtain wall on the two street sides. The architects designed the innovative glazing support details (right, below). Once-scattered divisions are housed on intermediate floors (typical floor plan, right), executive offices are on the top (fifth) floor and services and potential rentals are on the ground level. Interior spaces include executive reception (opposite page, top), typical drafting room with felt banner dividers, and a hallway.

TYPICAL FLOOR   N◁

Hedrich-Blessing

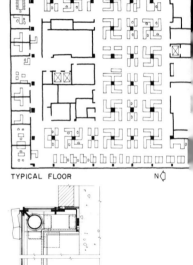

GLASS

HORIZONTAL WALL SECTION

7 Reuse of existing structures can fulfill a broad range of motives, and here is a case in point. The architect-client wanted to consolidate its scattered operations in a manner that would make the most economic sense yet still remain in central Detroit. SH&G's late chairman, Robert Hastings, was convinced that the resurgence of the city was just beginning, and that the firm's members should "be at the heart." They are a glistening reminder to the public of their presence.

SH&G began their new headquarters in 1971 by purchasing a 120,-000-square-foot loft building the firm had designed in 1910, and which met their program requirements of location, sound structure and floor area (three floors can be added in the future). Purchase price plus extensive renovation costs were estimated to total considerably less than the

Bob Wallace photos

cost of a new building—final costs were $31.66 per square foot in 1972–73. The first renovation procedure involved stripping the building to its concrete frame, retaining only stairwells and a freight elevator. The new plans were organized around the existing ability of respective floors to accommodate each of the firm's three working divisions. In a typical plan (opposite page) division executives are housed in offices on the north wall, and the large drafting rooms face the river views to the west. The columns—which were of various sizes and alignments—were furred out. Hung ceilings and carpeting were installed (the original wood floor could not be saved). An on-going art acquisition program has provided works of which the architects are duly proud. The artists include Motherwell, Frankenthaler and Lipshitz.

The most dramatic change is the essentially all-glass skin on the two street façades (a pre-energy crisis decision). The architects designed a tubular aluminum structural system to hold the glazing away from the exposed building frame. Five-foot by seven-foot sheets of bronze-tinted plate glass are held to polished aluminum supports, without stops, by silicone sealant. The x-shaped clamps held the glass while the sealant was curing, and provide extra support and a strong detail. Heating and cooling are provided by a variable volume system which utilizes light fixture heat in the winter, and the building's square shape coupled with two solid walls greatly reduce potential heat transfer.

SMITH, HINCHMAN & GRYLLS HEADQUARTERS, Detroit, Michigan. Owners, architects and engineers: *Smith, Hinchman & Grylls Inc.*

John G. Lewis, Jr. photos

8

The Kent-Valentine house in the heart of Richmond, with its oasis of magnolia trees and its grassy lawn, is a valuable asset to the city, and it has been acquired for preservation and adaptive reuse by the Garden Club of Virginia. Robert Stewart, an architect who encouraged the acquisition, found himself actively involved when the chance came to remodel what had been the old carriage house for his professional office. The small courtyard of the carriage house opens into a reception area and drafting room (top photos), from which a stairway leads to a second drafting room on the floor above (photo immediately above). Alterations to the existing building were minimal, and the genius of the design lies in Stewart's demonstrated ability to seize the moment and to recognize a pleasant and reusable building that had escaped others' notice.

OFFICE FOR ROBERT WELTON STEWART, Richmond, Virginia. Architect: *Robert Welton Stewart.* Contractor: *George Banducci.*

Stephen Dunham and Kiku Obata photos

9

HOK'S San Francisco office is in a part of the city between downtown and Telegraph Hill where renovation and adaptive use are the rage—an area characterized by large brick warehouse buildings ready to be turned to more glamorous commercial use. In this case the intention was to create a simple kind of space where there could be a heterogeneous mix of employees without the usual distinctions between front and back room. So the major part of the space is given over to one open office area (photo above) where members of the staff have their own work stations defined by low partitions. This large space is on the building perimeter, with exposure to natural light. On the inside wall there are three offices that offer more privacy (photo below) and a conference room.

OFFICE FOR HELLMUTH, OBATA & KASSABAUM, San Francisco, California. Architects: *Hellmuth, Obata & Kassabaum—project team: Gyo Obata, Dan Gale, Bill Valentine and Bob Stauder.* Contractor: *Balliet Brothers Construction Corporation.*

10

In remodeling this 60-year-old brick building in the Jackson Square district of San Francisco, all interior partitions were removed, and a new steel frame (to make the building earthquake-resistant) was introduced into the old structure. But the old brick walls and the posts, beams and joists of the original building were retained and incorporated into the remodeling. In its past the building had been used as a Chinese cigar factory, a restaurant and a souvenirs warehouse. The redesign of its interior was done to meet the needs of a publishing company, with many small offices around what is essentially one central open space but is actually a series of spaces which are open either up to the roof or down to the level below, providing an intricate and always changing spatial experience. No one opening, however, is the full height of the building, although from the reception area there is a view up through the building to the skylighted roof. Color, planes, space, light and line are the elements of the design; freestanding partitions, bridges, transparent walls, brightly painted exposed ducts and the varying openings are the means of implementing it.

SATURDAY REVIEW INDUSTRIES, INC., San Francisco, California. Architects: *Bull Field Volkmann Stockwell—Design Team: Daniel G. Volkmann, architect-in-charge; Herand M. Sarkissian, associate-in-charge; and Joseph D. Chance and James K. M. Cheng.* Engineers: *Anderson/Culley Associates, Peter A. Culley, principal-in-charge* (structural). Interiors: *Bull Field Volkmann Stockwell.* Contractor: *Lambert and Wells.*

Morley Baer photos except as noted

James K. M. Cheng

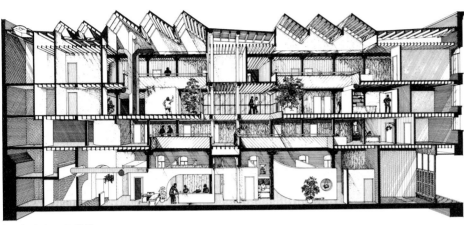

Drawing by James K. M. Cheng

While retaining the old posts and beams, the remodeling cut through portions of the floors to open up the interior in a series of open areas around which the small offices required by the client are ranged. All the free-standing partitions are painted white, as is the plywood encased steel truss behind the reception desk (left). From this point it is possible to look up through the entire height of the building thanks to the use of glass walls on the third level. The curved forms of partitions and of openings contrast strongly with the marked linearity of the other elements of the building.

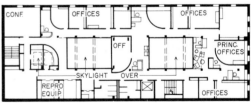

FOURTH FLOOR

THIRD FLOOR

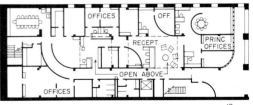

FIRST FLOOR

Although the remodeling was redone to the specific requirements of the publishing company, the solution has easily and successfully adapted to the needs of a firm of lawyers, which became the tenants upon cessation of publication of the *Saturday Review*. The tall windows in the principals' offices on the ground floor (above left) were one of the few changes made in the building exterior. The sandblasted old brick wall was allowed to show through in the conference room (center) and in most of the exterior perimeter offices. Bracing, needed for lateral resistance, is handled as an element of design wherever it was an unavoidable part of the remodeling (bottom).

11

When this building was a warehouse for the Crown-Zellerbach Paper Company, horse carts and old-fashioned trucks unloaded in the courtyard (right). Today San Franciscans come to the Irish Pub (bottom) and sit in the same courtyard sipping a pint. One Jackson Place was a herald of the tide of renovation which has seen nearly abandoned warehouses and factories turned into elegant commercial facilities—Ghiradelli Square, the Cannery, the Dancer-Fitzgerald-Sample offices, The Ice House. It quickly proved that urban renewal through preservation, not demolition, was a sound idea, both economically and esthetically.

Built in 1907 of brick salvaged from the earthquake and fire of the previous year, the existing complex was for San Francisco as old and outmoded as anything could be. For one thing, even though it was used as a whiskey warehouse after the repeal of Prohibition, the long alley leading to the truck dock was very inefficient for modern vehicles. For another, no self-respecting business would consider it as an address in the days when new office skyscrapers were shooting up all over town.

As in the case of Dancer-Fitzgerald-Sample, it was an advertising man, Joseph Weiner, who first saw the potential in the solid old structure. With industrial designer Walter Landor, he approached architect Lloyd Flood who has developed 100,000 square feet of luxury business space. Although One Jackson Place has special charm due to the scale of its shop-lined passage

Morley Baer photos

46

—not unlike a Venetian *calle*—
it shares certain advantages with
the nineteenth- and early twen-
tieth-century warehouse industrial buildings found in every
American town: solid construction and lots of high-ceilinged,
unobstructed floor space. Given
the relatively moderate cost of
installing modern conveniences
into these lofts, commercial
tenants can afford to rent much
more space than they could in
new construction. Furthermore,
the brick walls and timber truss
structures soaring above individual cubicles can give office
workers a sense of belonging.

Architect Flood, for in-
stance, spent approximately $20
per square foot (in 1968) and produced such elegant offices as
the one for U.S. Leasing Corp.
(center photo, left). Where fire
escapes were needed he installed steel balconies (right).
This is a solution very similar
to that used in the courtyard
of New York's rehabilitated
Westbeth Artists' Housing, another
open space formerly used for
truck loading. Wherever possible, Flood has exposed the timber structure (below left)
to the space below and has introduced devices in every office area to give it distinct
character: tiny patios off executive offices; planting areas;
even, in one case, a glass cage
cantilevered from the brick wall
to give greater spaciousness and
light. Corridors, too, are varied
by shallow glass bays which
either project or are indented
and which prevent the depress-
ing monotony of most office
building corridors.

ONE JACKSON PLACE, San Francisco,
California. Architects: *Lloyd Flood,
Bruce Beebe* (Phase 1). Engineers:
David Allan Welisch (structural); *West-
con Associates, Robert A. Wistort* (mech-
anical); *R. F. Darmsted & Associates*
(electrical). General contractor: *H. S.
Meinberger & Sons.*

12 Knorr and Elliott's new offices in San Francisco are in a fifty-year-old industrial building opportunely located in the increasingly desirable waterfront area of the city. The building was originally used as a feather factory, where chicken feathers were washed, cleaned and fluffed before being stuffed into pillows. (Hence graphics designer and artist Anne Knorr's delightful symbol for the building.) The requirements for the feather-cleaning operation were a lofty, large space in which the huge vats for feather washing could be located, and stairs, catwalks and decks for overseeing the vats. Knorr-Elliott have made the most of both the great volume of space at the center of the top floor and of the unusual system of stairs and decks left from the feather opera-

tion, changing little and using in unusual ways what they found in the building. It was necessary to strengthen the structure for earthquake resistance and to make a new fire wall on the north side; to build a stairway to serve the whole building; and to install an elevator. Some non-structural steel was removed. Otherwise, remodeling was a matter of decisions, cleaning and paint. The entire interior is white, color and pattern added by furnishings, art work (paintings by Anne Knorr, hanging sculpture by Ruth Asawa) and crafts (tapestry, banners).

THE FEATHER FACTORY, San Francisco, California. Architects: *Knorr-Elliott and Associates—Don Knorr, partner-in-charge.* Engineers: *Sexton, Fitzgerald & Kaplan* (structural). Contractor: *Greystone Builders.*

Robert Brandeis photos

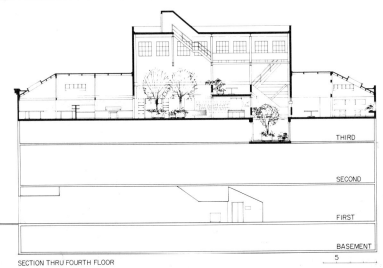

SECTION THRU FOURTH FLOOR

THIRD

SECOND

FIRST

BASEMENT

5

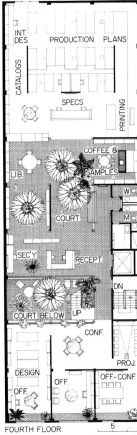

INT. DES.   PRODUCTION   PLANS

CATALOGS

SPECS

PRINTING

LIB.

COFFEE & SAMPLES

W

M

COURT

SEC'Y

RECEPT

DN

COURT BELOW UP

CONF.

DESIGN

OFF.

OFF.

OFF.-CONF.

PROJ.

FOURTH FLOOR   5

For all its essential openness, the plan produces places of clear definition: the reception area, just off the elevator "lobby" (above), the specification writers' desk, catalog and sample reference shelves (left) and the general library (right) evidence this. From the library the 35-foot height of the central section of the building's top floor is sheer space, interlaced by the dark charcoal lines of the steel structure and the catwalks and steel stairs that lead to the roof. Light pours into this space from high up on both north and south sides through large factory-type windows, increasing the apparent height and volume of the space. The ceiling of the main space and of the reception area, and the soffit of the catwalks, is of rough-finish Douglas fir laminated 2 by 6s, a warm texture and color in the overall scheme.

The conference room (top)—actually an existing catwalk widened to room size—is a spectacular location for discussions, suspended as it is in the 35-foot-high space. It overlooks on one side the reference library and on the other a court which reaches through to the building's third floor, where it provides daylight for rental offices on either side and acts as an open lounge for tenants on that floor. Low ceilinged areas at each end of the fourth floor are used as private and semi-private places: Don Knorr's office (including the design office) is at one end (center), and the drafting room (bottom) is at the other. The original beams and trusses, windows and skylights, were retained.

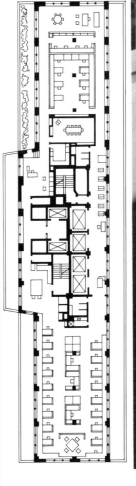

13

These offices occupy what is basically a loft space located in what was once called The Allied Arts Building, built in 1928 and modestly aspiring to the Art Deco style. This building, according to architect Kenneth Walker, represents a significant type of building stock in New York City that is very much under-utilized. "Part of the reason," he believes, " is that tenants look at this kind of building and think in terms of dropped ceilings and partitioned offices. To have accomplished this here would have been very expensive. But we made the most of what already existed and turned this building to our advantage."

In remodeling his loft, Walker capitalized on the inherent architectural characteristics of an industrial space—its high ceilings and large-scale industrially glazed windows. These surround the perimeter on all four sides and let in an unusual amount of natural light, while providing spectacular views of New York—the river, the U.N. and the cityscape.

The architects kept strictly to a vocabulary of industrial materials and components, with exposed conduits and ducts, factory-type lighting fixtures and a stark color scheme of black, red, white and grey. This severity offsets an unusually rich, varied and colorful collection of art which includes architectural sculpture, ornament and other relics from fine old New York buildings leveled by the wrecking ball.

As the plan indicates, the work spaces have been organized on the principles of open planning. This allows for a free flow of work, communication, interaction and the rapid regrouping of work teams as required. There are no private offices. Areas are divided by partitions, varying in height from 2 ft-6 in. to 7 ft. Grouped in the center core adjacent to the elevators are the only enclosed spaces—the conference room, the kitchen and the restrooms.

WALKER/GRAD INC. OFFICES, New York, N.Y. Architects: *Walker/Grad, Inc.—project designer: Lauder Bowden.* General contractor: *Jamco Construction Company.*

14

Until very recently, older industrial buildings did not attract developers of new commercial areas, yet these old buildings had and have great potential for new business neighborhoods, often with a built-in picturesqueness hard to achieve in other parts of cities. Their intrinsic values are often both esthetic and practical, for the warehouses of the late 19th century were often handsome buildings of architectural strength, as well as sturdy construction, and even their later counterparts of the early 20th century have virtues that the imaginative eye can find. Furthermore, these old buildings enclose a volume of space that cannot today be economically equaled, and they are, therefore, unique opportunities for conversion to new and contemporary uses.

San Francisco has been notable for such conversions in Ghirardelli Square, The Cannery, The Ice House and, much earlier, Jackson Square—all successful and profitable projects. The developer of the Ice House has now carried his experience and success across Market Street (the City's main thoroughfare) into a frankly industrial part of the city, where a 1916 block-size warehouse was converted to provide contract furnishings display-space. The Show Place!—as it is called—has been so successful that the same developer is now developing three handsome old brick buildings across the street into an office and display space complex called The Design Center.

With The Show Place! and The Design Center at one end of an extensive industrial area from which many businesses have already moved because of high land values or obsolete plants, and with a strong and good-looking office building project called China Basin Building as the other anchor, a new neighborhood is being created. Bold color and graphics, effective landscaping, and a new waterside plaza for sitting and eating, have transformed the neighborhood. Flexible interior space and access to freeways and transportation make it attractive to tenants from other parts of town.

CHINA BASIN BUILDING, San Francisco, California. Architects: *Robinson and Mills.* Engineers: *Bentley Engineers.* Landscape architect: *Frank Peccorini.* General contractor: *Turner Construction Co.*

THE SHOW PLACE! AND THE DESIGN CENTER, San Francisco, California. Owner: *Henry Adams & Company.* Architects: *Taylor/Huston.* Engineers: *GFDS Engineers* (structural); *David Ovenden & Associates* (electrical); *Harding-Lawson Associates* (soils); for The Design Center. General contractor: *Ralph Goldenberg, Inc.*

Robert Brandeis photos

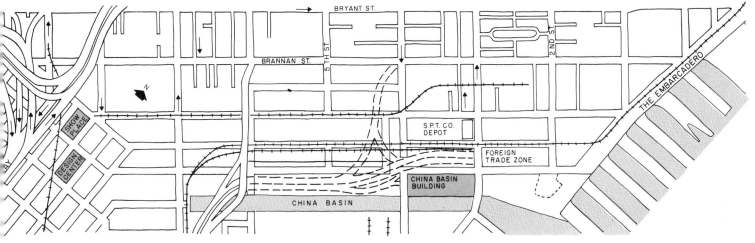

The projects illustrated here are all in San Francisco's south-of-Market-Street industrial area, where gradual rehabilitation of old, structurally sound buildings is giving new life to buildings long vacant. One of the first conversions from industrial to commerical use was The Show Place!, where contract furnishings companies can display their merchandise. Built in 1916, the one-time warehouse, imaginatively redesigned, has been successful enough to spur additional development in the block diagonally across the street. The large perspective drawing shows The Show Place! at right, and The Design Center—three handsome buildings currently being renovated for display space use—at left. Proposed for the empty lot between the first and second buildings is a skylighted landscaped court to serve as the focal point for the center. These four buildings are at one end of the area. At the other end is a huge structure, China Basin Building, 825 feet long, once a storage and distribution plant. In remodeling it, the architects broke its massive scale by dividing it into four quadrants, each separately entered, and painted the exterior a deep blue.

15

Unused space in a company-owned warehouse was transformed into the bright, colorful offices shown here, using a small budget (equal to three years' rent of the previously occupied offices) and ingenious design. Most of the budget was used for mechanical and electrical improvements—acoustical control, air conditioning and lighting. With the exception of new chairs and new work station–conference tables, the furnishings are from the old offices, brought into harmony with the new surroundings by hiding them behind bold Marimekko banners and the new work station partitions. The open plan, of which the freestanding work stations are an important element (serving as partitions between spaces assigned to middle management) was accepted by employees with some misgivings during the design stage. But actual experience with the good lighting, bright colors and spatial volume of the new quarters has dispelled initial doubts. Colors—red on trusses, yellow on ducts, and green on one wall—derive from the familiar colors of company advertisements; graphics, using the company logo, evoke simultaneously nostalgia and contemporaneity.

OFFICE FOR COCA-COLA, San Francisco, California. Architects and interior designers: *John O'Brien/John Armstrong, Barry Brukoff Interiors, Inc., associated.* Contractor: *Thomas Scadden Inc.*

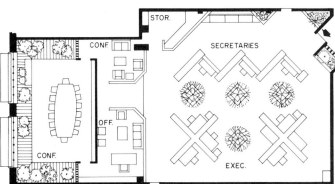

Light in the old warehouse was from skylights which did not fit the design for the new offices. Canvas awnings hide them and admit softly diffused light throughout the work space.

Jeremiah Bragstad photos

Jack Stock Studios photos

16

When the City of New Haven was planning the Dixwell urban renewal area, the question was debated, "Should Eastern Press and other non-conforming uses be allowed to remain in a residential neighborhood?" Business was growing rapidly for Eastern Press Inc. and the 40-year-old building was in good condition, though it needed expansion. Supported by the owner of Eastern Press Inc., Ray Johnson, his architect Earl Carlin and others, the planners who believed that urban neighborhoods should not be rigidly compartmented by zoning uses won the debate. Given this theoretical victory, the architects had still to translate it into the physical form of a building that the people living in the neighborhood would find compatible.

Access and entrances. The site is trapezoidal, separated from Goffe Street to the south by a greenbelt strip which the City retained for future widening and planting. The location of the existing building and internal functions determined that the entrance drive and parking lot be to the south. A single curb cut on Orchard Street serves where two had been necessary for the original plant. Parking is clearly differentiated from truck movement, and the loading area is screened off by a row of jack pines, which will soon form a dense hedge. There are few pedestrians on this side of Orchard Street; the movement is on the east side around John Johansen's new two-story housing project.

The architects clearly differentiated loading dock, personnel entrance and pub-

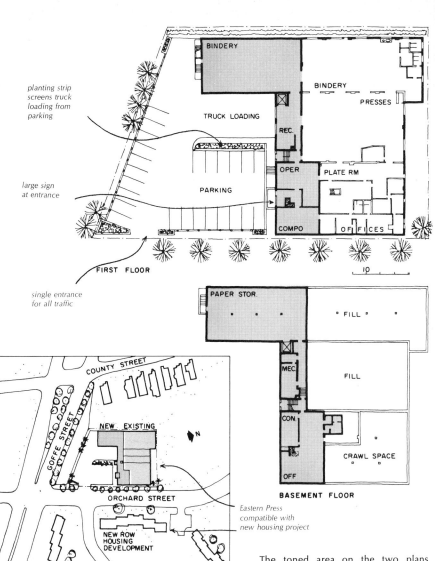

planting strip screens truck loading from parking

large sign at entrance

FIRST FLOOR

single entrance for all traffic

BASEMENT FLOOR

Eastern Press compatible with new housing project

The toned area on the two plans above indicates the 10,900-square-foot addition to the existing plant, built in the 1920s. The patterned block used for the addition was designed by the architects and was carried around the front and north side of the existing building to join new with old. Norman Ives' banner dominates the main entrance (above, right) and adds bright accents to the main office area (right). The three wood-framed residences that appear in the photo of the old Eastern Press (left) were torn down by the New Haven Redevelopment Agency, making room for the building's expansion.

lic entrance. The public entrance is marked by graphics designer Norman Ives' giant porcelain-enameled panel, a pattern of red and white triangles suggesting an "E", which has the gaiety of a medieval knight's banner and somewhat the same purpose. Two more material functions are also incorporated within the sign: The horizontal part of its support keeps rain off the entrance and the sign itself shades the glass-walled lobby from the southwest sun.

Plan and massing. One story in an industrial plant equals two in a house. This relationship was already established by the existing building and its neighbors (see above), and was maintained in the design of its expansion, to compatibly relate Eastern Press to a new two-story housing project (designed by John Johansen) across the street. Painted concrete blocks of special design are intended to echo the materials used in the Johansen project, and are carried across the face of the old building to unify the composition. A six-foot-diameter helical stair in the lobby leads downward to offices, in an interesting reversal of conventional movement. Additional work and storage areas are provided on the lower floor. The lack of windows in the bindery must bother the claustrophobic, but there are compensating advantages for air-conditioning and for the exterior form.

Expansion. Ray Johnson started Eastern Press by accident. In 1958 he sold a press to the editors of the Yale Daily News. They soon learned that printing as well as editing a paper was more time-consuming than their studies could permit. Johnson took over printing their paper and did it so well that more and more printing work was brought to him, including extensive lithography for advertising.

He cannot expand further on this site. Johnson has chosen to grow by establishing branches, and there are now three in addition to this main plant, each with a semi-autonomous management.

EASTERN PRESS INC. New Haven. Architects: *Carlin, Pozzi & Associates—Peter Millard, associate.* Engineers: *Henry A. Pfisterer* (structural); *Hill & Harrigan* (mechanical). Graphic design: *Norman Ives.* Contractor: *Jaybe Construction Company.*

Bill Maris photos

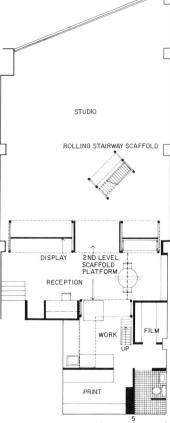

STUDIO

ROLLING STAIRWAY SCAFFOLD

DISPLAY | 2ND LEVEL SCAFFOLD PLATFORM

RECEPTION

WORK | FILM

UP

PRINT

5

17

This arresting photography studio was converted from double-height loft space on Lower Fifth Avenue in New York City. The reception, conference and photo processing areas are painted white and fitted out with metal scaffolding adapted by the architects to a variety of special uses. On the mezzanine level, scaffold bridges lead to storage areas, a small office and model change room. Throughout the interior, the steel pipe provides flexible, clamp-on lighting set ups and varied possibilities for display.

The pipe scaffolding has a strong linear quality that moves the eye to every corner of the space and back again. The elements are inexpensive and demountable, and, in many cases, easily rearranged as new needs arise in the future.

PHOTOGRAPHER'S STUDIO, New York City. Owner: *Joseph Reynolds.* Architects: *Mayers & Schiff;* contractor: *Glenn Partition Company.*

18

Central Avenue in Pawtucket, Rhode Island (photo left) is scarcely a dream site. Run-down at the heels, with some 19th century factory buildings mixed with cheap-as-possible cinder block warehouse space, some stores from the last era when glass block was groovy and lots of parking lots, it is—alas —typical of just-outside-downtown in a hundred American cities.

Teknor Apex' program for the remodeling of its Central Avenue corporate offices was similarly modest. The need was for new office space—"utilitarian, inexpensive, nothing ostentatious"; and since the company produces products only for resale to other manufacturers, "concerns regarding public image are limited," as indeed they are often in the plans of industry for its building projects.

Says architect Warren Platner: "We rather enjoy the task of trying to make something of distinction from very little, especially if there is something inherited to respect."

The starting point for the remodeling was: 1. The 19th-century factory building shown below—which behind patched-on exhaust ducts and decades of grime did offer "something inherited to respect" in its old brick, arched windows, and New England forthrightness, and . . . 2. The completely featureless cinder block structure next door (see "before" photo on

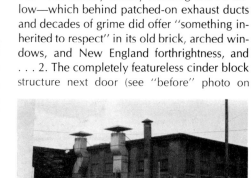

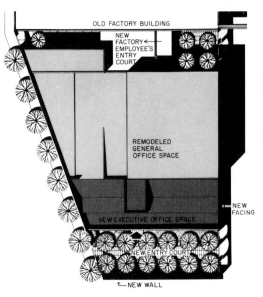

page 61) which adjoined the plant, was owned by the client, and had been used as a discount retail outlet.

Until the remodeling, Teknor Apex' office space had been contained in the factory building, and a combined need for more production space and more office space led to the job.

Platner's solution to the space problem was to remodel the cinder block building for general office space (top of plan) and add a small, one-story addition beyond for executive offices (bottom of plan) which opens through an all-glass wall (photo below) to a tree-shaded court. The planning of the new offices was, of course, a fairly routine design problem. What is not routine is the totally new character of space and environment and order created by Platner and his design team.

The top photo at left shows that the cinder block building, to be used for general office space, was given new windows (simply punched through the cinder block walls and given the arch form borrowed from the plant) and refaced in brick matched as closely as possible to the factory. The brick chosen was an inexpensive common brick made by the same producer who provided the brick for the plant nearly 100 years ago.

The unsightly yard between the plant and the office building (again, see photo left) was landscaped and semi-enclosed with the arched wall shown in the photos. This provided a handsome new entry court for the plant employees.

As the top photo shows, the wall continues at the lower level of the new executive-office wing, extends past to form the arched entry to the main entrance (both bottom photos) and terminates in a freestanding wall at the property line. This second larger court is paved in matching blocks and planted with plane trees and euonymus. Platner's conscious decision (with the client's approval) to open this courtyard to the neighborhood was accepted by the neighborhood: it is now a busy and appreciated mid-block passage. The reflective-glass curtain wall assures privacy for company executives while giving them a pleasant and controlled view—and doubling the apparent size of the court.

The buttressed brick wall at the right in the photo below is freestanding, simply separating the courtyard from the not-too-handsome commercial buildings beyond.

The interiors are simple and spartan, and of common and inexpensive materials, but—as is characteristic of Platner's work—detailed with great care and precision. In the remodeled section (photos below and bottom right) the retail-store space ("before" photo at left) was stripped to its wood structure and concrete floor. The multitude of columns in the space was mostly incorporated in new partitions, which are framed and trimmed in red oak, and are about half clear glass and half pre-finished hardboard with a random-groove pattern. Conference-room spaces are glass-enclosed, but have narrow-slat blinds which can be lowered for privacy when needed. Carpeting is on-slab, and the ceiling is a conventional hung ceiling with "the least expensive lighting fixture made by the manufacturer. We like the fixture,"

Platner says, "because being the cheapest, it was also the plainest and simplest." About 50 per cent of the furniture was moved from the old office and repainted to match new steel furniture designed for the manufacturer by Platner some years ago.

In the new executive-office space, the same simple finishes were used, though, of course, spaces are more generous and the furniture more luxurious (mostly wood—and again designed for the manufacturers by the architect). As the top photos at right show, most of these offices share the view of the entry courtyard, but have narrow-slat blinds because the space faces west. In the entry lobby (top right) a skylight and a panel of wood parquet are intended to create "a sense of location."

Construction of this new space is (to save

money) short span, with columns of square steel tubing and light weight trusses. But again Platner achieved some elegance with such simple devices as incandescent wall-washers and a foot-wide strip of parquet as a border around the carpet.

Total cost of the job was $32.13 a square foot—$26.60 for all building work—renovation and new construction including sprinklers and air conditioning; $5.53 for all floor covering, furniture refinishing, and new furniture.

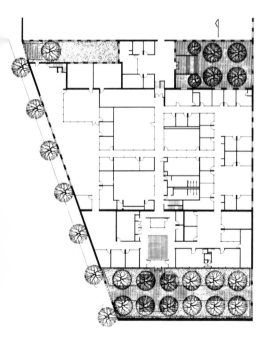

TEKNOR APEX COMPANY OFFICES, Pawtucket, Rhode Island. Architects: *Warren Platner Associates Architects—associates of Warren Platner on this project: Jesse Lyons, project architect; Bob Brauer, project designer, Bill Smith and Lee Ahlstrom, furnishings.* Graphics consultant: *Jill Mitchell.* Engineer: *Alonzo B. Reed, Incorporated.* General contractor: *Owner.*

Renovation and Remodeling for Selling and Shopping

The transformation of an old warehouse or factory into a glamorous, colorful collection of shops and restaurants is a late Twentieth century phenomenon—with good but unlikely precedents like the exotic oriental bazaar and the sophisticated European shopping arcade. Unlike such precedents, where need and purpose gave rise to form, this new type of commercial venture is housed in existing buildings whose size, materials, volume and space have been determinants and conditioners of outward form and spatial character. It must be said, however, that this has not been without benefit to the end result, for out of the stimulus of using the old, have been created individual and unusual designs of exceptional attraction to patronage. From patronage comes success, and success spells profit. Most of the renovated, restored, and remodeled commercial and industrial complexes of this kind have been both successful and profitable.

The economic viability of one old building saved from demolition eases the way for saving another, and if it is in the same block as the first, to preserving a neighborhood. There is a special value to a community in such a project, for it can revitalize a decaying area and it certainly works to retain the scale as well as the look of the past.

On the following pages are shown complexes and small shops, all with the common denominator of being housed in old buildings successfully rehabilitated and remodeled with benefit to the economy, the community, and to the quality of the urban scene.

Many an old building is good for renewed life when modernized to meet current standards or new concepts for its original function. Although sentiment may sometimes play a part in the desire to retain an old building (especially on college campuses), it is more likely common sense that dictates its renovation and continued use.

1

Ghirardelli Square, San Francisco's most famous preservation project, is a collection of old and new buildings focussed on the 19th century-early 20th century buildings of a chocolate factory. These, and one even older structure, had stood on a block-sized site on the waterfront overlooking the Golden Gate, generally unnoticed except for the aromas that came from the manufacture of ground chocolate and candy bars. When the company moved to a new plant in another city, the property was bought by San Francisco businessman William M. Roth with the specific intent of preserving the old buildings —atonement, he said, for his own lack of action in time to save the Montgomery Block, an elegant 1851 office building on whose site the Transamerica Building now stands. Roth's act of civic conscience proved important to the overall development of the northern waterfront, since it saved this section from the then legally possible construction of high rise buildings, and also maintained the scale and character which it had had for nearly a century.

The new owner of the property engaged architects and landscape architects to design the complex of shops, restaurants and theaters which has stirred many to envy and some to imitation. Ghirardelli's special charm is a subtle mixture of buildings, outdoor spaces, art objects, colorful wares and people. It is, above all, a place for people—a place in which there is great variety of activity: shopping, eating, strolling, sitting in the sun, or just enjoying the visual entertainment of the passing scene and the view of San Francisco Bay.

The site slopes steeply toward the Bay and Victorian Park, a broad expanse of lawn (with a cable-car turnaround at the end of the line), and the slope makes possible a parking garage—essential near such a tourist attraction as Ghirardelli Square has become—under the plaza but with easy access from two streets.

The buildings enclose two large plazas and many small intimate open spaces—decks, terraces, balconies, wide landings on stairways —which serve in varied ways. Some become parts of restaurants for outdoor eating, some are transition points between levels of the complex. Landscaping is simple, and is used to differentiate levels and spaces as much as to enhance the visual environment, introducing color in flower-filled planters.

GHIRARDELLI SQUARE, San Francisco, California. Architects: *Wurster, Bernardi & Emmons.* Engineers: *Gilbert Forsberg Diekmann Schmidt* (structural); *G. L. Gendler & Associates* (mechanical). Landscape architects: *Lawrence Halprin & Associates.* Design consultant: *John Matthias.* Contractor: *Swinterton & Walberg.*

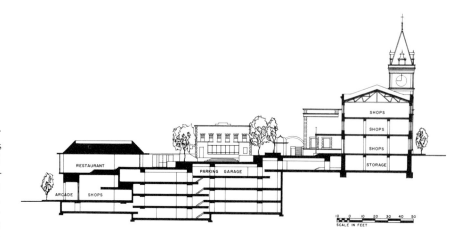

SCALE IN FEET

So well handled is the scale, character and overall design of the new buildings that the average visitor is almost if not entirely unaware that this complex is actually a skillful blending of old and new. The new buildings have been incorporated into the complex with becoming modesty, several achieving this in a quasi-recall of architect William Mooser's 1915 Tower Building and Chocolate Factory (right), as in the Wurster Building (above), named for its architect. Others, like the pavilions on the plaza, use a different idiom and different materials in a surprisingly compatible way.

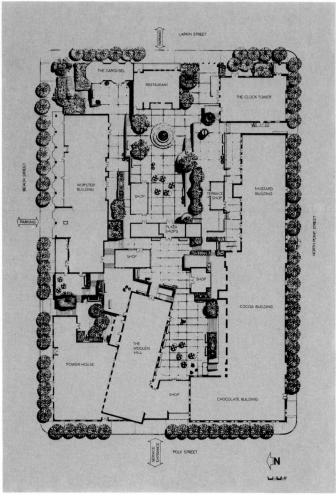

A festive, holiday air pervades Ghirardelli Square, especially in its open spaces, through which every visitor passes. These terraced and landscaped places are scaled to create a sense of intimacy which quite belies the actual number of people present a one time in one space. Some of the restaurants open directly from the plazas; others are located off landings of broad steps leading into the plaza from the street; still others, on the upper floors of the taller buildings, overflow to balconies with superb views of the Bay. Exteriors of the old buildings were cleaned and repaired where necessary; otherwise they were left unchanged. Interiors were replanned to accommodate many small shops. Sculpture by such well-known San Francisco sculptors as Ruth Asawa and Beniamino Bufano is an important element in character of the complex.

2

The two buildings shown in the photo (upper left) are situated on Boston's Long Wharf and linger as a link with the city's 18th century past. The larger of the two, the old Custom House, has already been placed on the National Register of historic places, but by 1966 was largely vacant and neglected. Boston architects Anderson Notter Associates were commissioned to convert the four-story granite building into 27 luxury apartment units. Transverse masonry walls actually separated the structure into nine separate buildings—each with a full attic. The architects pierced these walls with new arches to let corridors through. Modern egress stairs and a new elevator shaft were installed. New electrical services, central heating, sprinklers and intercom system were also installed. The massive timbers framing the roof were exposed in the attic duplexes and old masonry walls were cleaned with care. Because of the building's configuration, each apartment is spatially unique and looks out over the old Boston waterfront in a broad vista of water and shipping.

The smaller building, adjacent to the Custom House, was purchased by a West Coast restaurant chain that specializes in broiled seafood and steak. Because of the restrictions placed on the project by the Historic District, the exteriors were retained very nearly intact. Using the same technique they employed in the Custom House, Anderson Notter cut through transverse walls of the three existing bays and built new arches from old brick removed to make the openings. Brick walls were sandblasted and old timber joists were exposed and cleaned. The lowest level is used as a cocktail lounge; the second floor and mezzanine serve as dining spaces. A manager's office and support spaces occupy the old attic and create the uppermost partial level seen in the section (top right).

Both conversions were executed with very considerable design concern and with respect for the virtues of the original structures. The result is that two historic buildings, suffering from long neglect, are now restored to usefulness and a disintegrating portion of the city is starting to feel the quickening pulse of new waterfront activity.

CUSTOM HOUSE BLOCK AND CHART HOUSE RESTAURANT, Boston, Massachusetts. Architects: *Anderson Notter Associates, Inc.* Engineers: *Arthur Choo Associates* (structural); *W. N. Peterson Associates, Inc.* (mechanical); *Joseph V. Herosy* (electrical). Contractor: *Stoneholm Construction Company.*

MEZZANINE FLOOR

FIFTH FLOOR

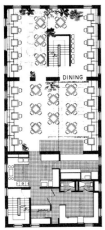

SECOND FLOOR

GROUND FLOOR   5

The three structural bays that
formed the original building are still
visible in the plans although
the architects pierced the transverse
walls with new arched openings.
Restaurant use, to conform with local
codes, was restricted to the
middle two floors, and the street floor
is used as a cocktail lounge.

The detailing of new work
throughout is consistent but not fussy
so that it matches, in spirit at least,
the shims and ad hoc character of
the original framing,
much of which was concealed before
renovation. Nothing seems quite plumb
in the old building and the
architects made a virtue
of these eccentricities in the
renovation.

3

Larimer Square is a block of 19th-century buildings adjacent to downtown Denver and a redevelopment area. The old masonry walls of the buildings have been reconstructed and left exposed instead of, as too often happens, being hidden behind a veneer of smooth new materials. Architectural details such as cornices, arches and columns have, however, been restored, but this has been done only where these details were originally a part of the facade, thus maintaining the true character and flavor of the building. On the rear of the buildings, where there had been no pretense of architecture, the architect felt free to incorporate new arched or flat window openings and doorways, and to open up a mid-block walkway onto which shops (like the tie shop, right, with its simple contemporary design) open. Old and new are juxtaposed without disharmony.

LARIMER SQUARE, Denver, Colorado. Owner: *Larimer Square Associates*. Architects: *Langdon Morris, associate partner, RNL, Inc.* Engineers: *Vernon Winkel* (structural); *John Blank* (mechanical); *Harold Dyer* (electrical). General contractor: *Kraft Building Contractors*.

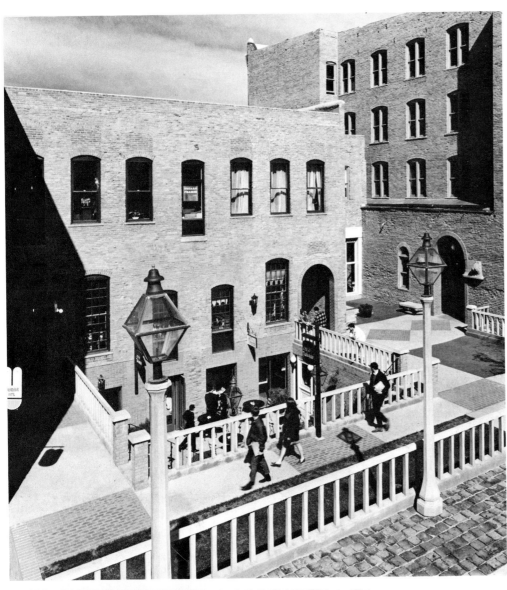

New masonry walls were integrated with the old walls to create a sunken court which is used for outdoor dining at the below-grade cafe. New rectangular openings which the architect felt free to use on this rear façade since it had no architectural pretensions, make a subtle contrast with the old arched windows above.

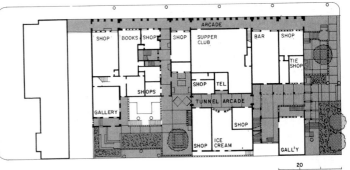

4

The Cannery in San Francisco is a complex of shops and restaurants in an old three-story loft building originally used as the Del Monte Fruit Cannery. A survivor of the 1906 earthquake, the building today survives only in its exterior walls; everything else is new, designed for its new function as a shopping center. What has resulted is a collection of small shops and a variety of restaurants of various sizes, connected by a continuously interesting system of walks, corridors, steps, escalator, balcony decks and a glass-walled outside elevator. The scale is neither grand nor intimate, but something in between—right for a public place and, at the same time, for the ordinary activities of people. The architects, free to design the interior of the old structure in any way they wished, chose to work with the same material—brick—and with details of the original building. The complex is entered from three points: direct to Cannery Walk, between the two buildings which the architects made of the original one; and from either end of Cannery Street, a landscaped mall between The Cannery and Wharfside, an old warehouse restored as an office building, which makes an appropriate background for the mall and its activities.

THE CANNERY, San Francisco, California. Architects: *Esherick, Homsey, Dodge and Davis.* Engineers: *Rutherford & Chekene* (structural); *Edward Shinn & Associates* (electrical); *K.T. Belotelkin & Associates* (mechanical). Landscape architects: *Thomas Church & Associates.* Consultants: *Richard C. Peters* (lighting); *Marget Larsen* (graphics); *Walter W. Soroka* (acoustical); *Bert Marshall* (food service). General contractor: *Greystone Builders, Inc.*

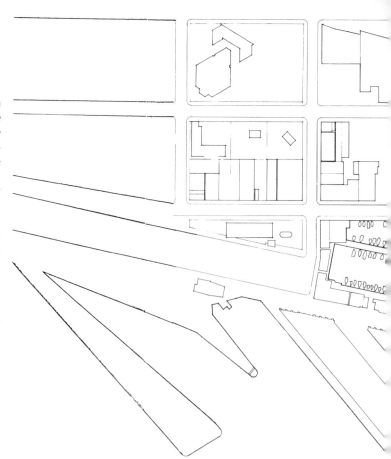

George Dippel-Intrinsics

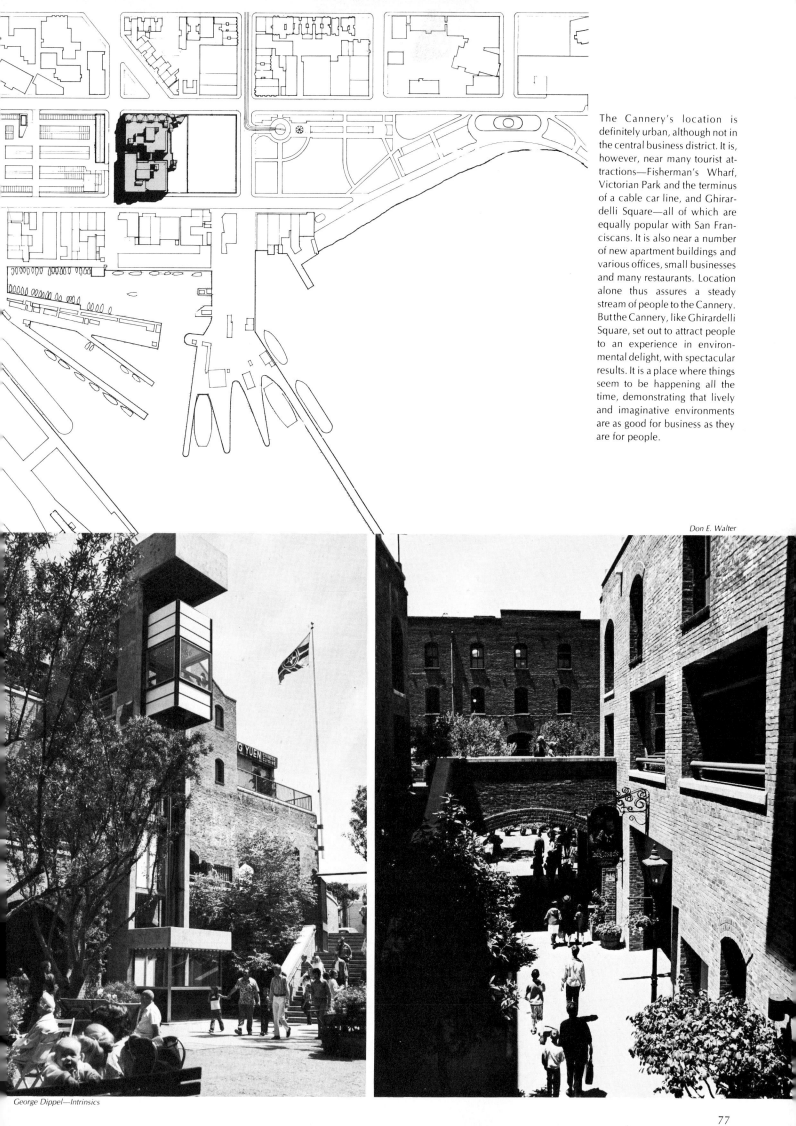

The Cannery's location is definitely urban, although not in the central business district. It is, however, near many tourist attractions—Fisherman's Wharf, Victorian Park and the terminus of a cable car line, and Ghirardelli Square—all of which are equally popular with San Franciscans. It is also near a number of new apartment buildings and various offices, small businesses and many restaurants. Location alone thus assures a steady stream of people to the Cannery. But the Cannery, like Ghirardelli Square, set out to attract people to an experience in environmental delight, with spectacular results. It is a place where things seem to be happening all the time, demonstrating that lively and imaginative environments are as good for business as they are for people.

Don E. Walter

George Dippel—Intrinsics

The Cannery's architecture was more clearly visible just after completion of its "reconstruction" than it is now that shrubs and trees have matured. With this lusher vegetation has come, however, an environment of almost Mediterranean exuberance, particularly in the open spaces at ground level but augmented by the constant movement of people through the several levels of the buildings. The stark forms and austere detail adapted from the original Cannery walls are strong elements in the Walk (below, left, and above, right), as the outside elevator shaft (top left) is in the mall.

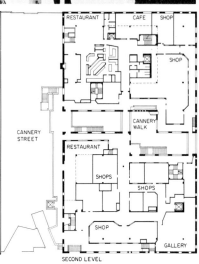

SECOND LEVEL

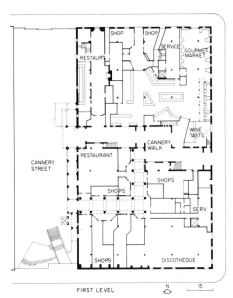

FIRST LEVEL

5

Old Town, a commercial and fine arts center in Los Gatos, California, some 50 miles south of San Francisco, preserves and imaginatively exploits the scale and character appropriate to a small town. Where a shopping center of typical dimensions would have violated the particular quality of the area, Old Town fits right in to the town and contributes its own kind of visual and cultural delight to the community. Admittedly a specialty center, Old Town has exceeded the developer's most optimistic expectations so that the first phase, shown here, will soon be augmented by phases two and three. The building around which the center is being developed is a 1923 Mission-style school building sold by the district in 1957. Remodeling the building was not inexpensive, says the architect, but it not only netted greater height and more space than new construction could have provided, but it preserved a community landmark. The architects added wood decks, trellises and balconies, and extended the roof in some portions to provide covered access to upper level shops. The conference room—a new building visible in the photograph at bottom—is available to the community for functions and meetings and is a part of the promotional activities of the center. These are generally cultural in nature, and attract large numbers of potential shoppers. An outdoor amphitheater at the rear of the old school building is used for summer programs. Future expansion of the center will include remodeling of some of the old buildings in the vicinity: an old mill will be restored as a mill and a bakery; a church will be remodeled to resemble the old railroad station and will be used as a banquet room.

OLD TOWN, Los Gatos, California. Owner-developer: *Max Walden*. Architects: *Frank Laulainen & Associates*. Engineers: *Honholdt and Sweany* (civil). Landscape consultant: *Paul McMullen*. General contractors: *James A. Mason* (exterior work); *Frans A. Laulainen* (interior work).

Joshua Freiwald photos

Shops, studios with artists at work, restaurants, an outdoor amphitheater and a theater-auditorium make up Los Gatos Old Town, a center of specialty shops whose main building is a remodeled schoolhouse. The old school auditorium-theater (shown, remodeled and with a new bandstand addition, immediately below) is now used for conferences, exhibitions, musical and dramatic events. Shop exteriors and signs were controlled by a group headed by the architect, who was also responsible for many shop interiors.

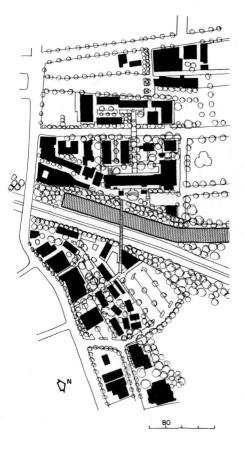

Social and economic values gradually passed this 70-year-old masonry structure by. It began as a stable and a turn-around shed for horse-drawn trolleys, was later converted to a parking structure, then finally drifted into a period of long neglect. In the ordinary course of events it would have been demolished, but its location on Harvard Square—on a prime, block-long site next to the Holyoke Center—was its salvation. Careful analysis of its potential as a retail center encouraged the Wasserman Development Corporation to commission architects ADD Inc (Architecture Design Development) to prepare plans for the building's renovation and conversion to a mini shopping mall.

The Garage's transformation into a retail complex was skillful and sensitive. The exterior masonry walls, lovingly enriched with details, were carefully preserved. So were the interior concrete ramps. Bricked up windows, blind arches and closed entrances were reopened. Windows painted for opacity were replaced. A fourth level, framed in steel, was added to the top of the old structure but was clad in brick matched to the color and texture of the lower three floors.

The finished project produced about 70,-000 square feet of commercial space and cost nearly $3 million. The basement includes a 9,000-square-foot restaurant, a hi-fi store and a camera shop. The new upper level contains two concert clubs known as Performance Centers I and II. The levels between, strung together by the system of existing ramps, form an elaborate and spatially arresting series of small shops and boutiques (a "Persian Bazaar" the architects call it) that offer an extended range of merchandise to a predominately young clientele. Because of the openness of the space, individual tenants intermingle visually without the usual barriers of door and wall. The long sight lines that result tend to lead the browser on and to intensify his desire to examine merchandise. In the strongly pedestrian ambience of Harvard Square, this seems especially appropriate. As with other buildings in this section, this once-derelict building has been reintegrated usefully into a city's urban fabric.

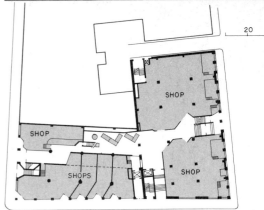

THE GARAGE, Cambridge, Massachusetts. Owner: *Wasserman Development Corporation.* Architects: *ADD Inc.* Engineers: *Irwin Cantor* (structural); *Bernard F. Greene* (mechanical). Graphic consultants: *Michael Sand and Associates.* Contractor: *Jacet Construction Corporation.*

Steve Rosenthal photos

7

The Ice House—in actuality not one building but two—was originally just what its name indicates, an ice warehouse. Built in 1914, the two buildings, one seven stories high, the other five stories, have been converted into showrooms for contract furnishings with little change to either exterior or interior. In fact, the only addition to the buildings which is visible from the street is a five-story-glass-enclosed bridge which dramatically links the two buildings. The red brick exteriors, handsome but not ornate, were cleaned, and new entrances were provided off the alley between the two buildings. Inside a new stairwell connects the main floor with the third floor.

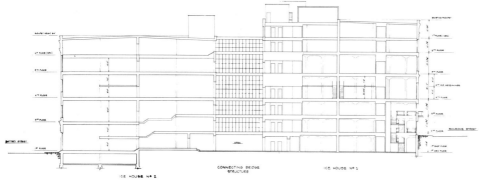

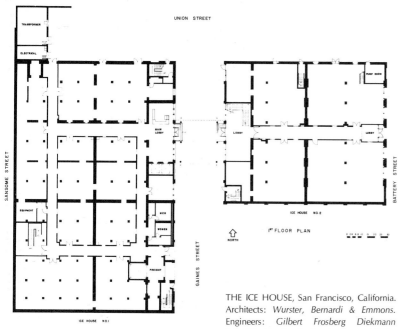

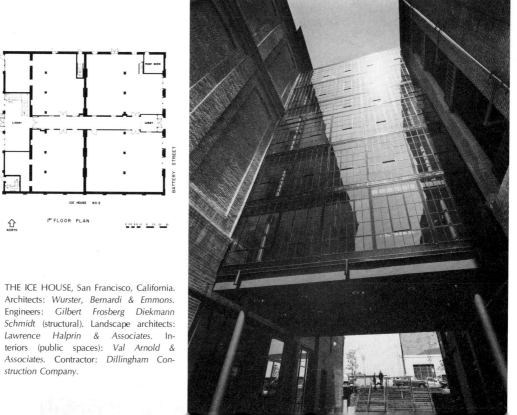

THE ICE HOUSE, San Francisco, California. Architects: *Wurster, Bernardi & Emmons.* Engineers: *Gilbert Frosberg Diekmann Schmidt* (structural). Landscape architects: *Lawrence Halprin & Associates.* Interiors (public spaces): *Val Arnold & Associates.* Contractor: *Dillingham Construction Company.*

8

Pioneer Square is Seattle's most historic area, the place from which developed the modern city of Seattle. The name applies to both the small triangular park in front of the Pioneer Building, with the graceful pergola marking the entrance to the old fashioned public rest room, the totem pole, and the benches for the Skid Rowers (the name originated here), and to the 52-acre area which contains a treasury of three-to six-story 1890 buildings, most salvageable for continued use and many of architectural interest. The renascence of the area dates from the late 1960's, though efforts to preserve it were going on for at least a decade before that, in all of which architects were prime movers. Finally in 1970 the city established the Pioneer Square Historic District, with a board to oversee its conservation, and in 1973 designated it a Special Review District with further control of land use with its confines. Because the buildings replace those of an earlier period destroyed in the Great Fire of 1889, there is a remarkable architectural consistency in them, but this is offset by the variety in the district itself. The economic benefits to the city and to investors of what has taken place in the Pioneer Square district is a phenomenon of more than passing interest, and represents an enlightened citizenry recognizing just in time its own heritage, and an equally enlightened government responsive to and contributing in the public sector.

The Pioneer Building—one of Seattle's most significant buildings, architecturally and historically—dates from the period immediately after the 1889 fire which completely destroyed the city's first business center. Most of the buildings had been of wood; those that replaced them were of brick and stone. For several decades after its completion in 1892 the six-story red brick Pioneer Building was the city's most desirable office address. It lost its prominence, as did other buildings in the Pioneer Square district, when business moved to cheaper land and larger sites to the north and, like the other buildings in the abandoned financial center, began a long deterioration. The handsome Pioneer lost most of its tenants and for many years was a shelter for derelicts.

Early in 1973 a group of investors bought the building, rehabilitated it for office use and restored its prestige as a business address. The exterior was sandblasted, the terracotta decorative detail was cleaned and repaired, and the structure was strengthened where necessary. Inside, the two skylighted courts fully restored, again give distinction to the building. Even the ceramic tile in the common area on the first floor has been cleaned and repaired to bring back the original appearance of the interior. The original elevator shafts, where the first electric elevators in Seattle were used, and the handsome stairway with its fine wood banister, connecting all the floors, have been restored to their early elegance.

Considerable modernization was, of course, necessary. The building has been air conditioned; new wiring has been installed; and new plumbing and heating systems were included in the rehabilitation. A sprinkler system is an important addition, and made possible retention of the interior courts.

THE PIONEER BUILDING, Seattle, Washington. Owners/developers: *Pioneer Investment Company*. Architects: *Ralph Anderson and Partners*. Engineers: *Olsen & Ratti* (structural). Contractor: *Fleming Sorenson Construction Company*.

The Maynard Building, one block south of the Pioneer Building, was completed in the same year—1892—and it too figured in the city's history, serving as the financial center during the Alaska gold rush of 1897–98, and providing on its upper floors handsome offices for the city's professional firms. But even the Maynard proved vulnerable to the decay that set in after 1900. In the various uses to which it was put, it suffered considerable mutilation of its fine oak panelling and other interior detailing. Finally, it succumbed: for 30 years its only occupants were pigeons.

As the Pioneer Square Historic District development gained momentum, the building's good qualities became obvious. Its imposing architectural statement, both inside and out, its essentially good condition, and its excellent location made preservation and continuing use very desirable. Two courageous developers bought it, repaired the spalled stone exterior, replaced damaged details and brought the building back to its original appearance.

Although repairing the exterior required care and skill, the interior had its own demands. Unusually fine oak panelling, an integral part of the building's interior character, had been defaced in some places and was completely missing in others. Painstakingly, the architects pieced together parts and replaced details to achieve a sensitive restoration of the original public areas. A new elevator cab was designed to fit in the original shaft and to retain the "gold cage" look, and the carved oak banister of the stairway that wraps around the shaft was restored. The only significant change is the new circulation pattern on the lobby floor, where a corridor connecting the main entrance with a new doorway around the corner passes a glass-enclosed interior court, an attractive feature among the shops on this level. Where new mechanical work has been incorporated, it has been done with a minimum of visible effect.

THE MAYNARD BUILDING, Seattle, Washington. Owners: *Alan Black and Richard White.* Architects: *Olson Walker Associates.* Engineers: *Olsen & Ratti* (structural). Contractor: *Fleming Sorenson Construction Company.*

The Grand Central Hotel Building was a lively landmark in the days of the Alaska gold rush but when that was over, it lost caste and patronage and gradually decayed in reputation and physical condition. The building was bought in 1971 by two developers and an architect (Ralph Anderson, whose earlier purchase and restoration of several old buildings in the district had initiated the Pioneer Square renascence), rechristened Grand Central on the Park and returned to its original use as an office building. The new owners gave it needed modern amenities and altered it only slightly, and with commendable sensitivity, to allow for more public use of its street level, making it, in the process, an important catalyst in the success of the Pioneer Square district.

Except for cleaning the exterior and changing the store windows at street level to give consistent scale to the street facades, and the addition of a handsome iron grille and gateway entrance, little needed to be done on the outside of the building. The original cornice had been removed after an earthquake, and no attempt was made to replace it. The parapet, however, was strengthened with a continuous bond beam. The structure also needed strengthening to bring it up to code.

The major alteration at street level was the creation of an arcade concourse which connects First Avenue, the district's main street, and the new city-financed Occidental Park and which is a prime attraction for visitors to the area. The wide brickwalled arcade is meeting place and resting point, entrance and passageway. Off it open shops and cafes; a restaurant with a glass-enclosed pavilion projecting into the park; and stairways, one leading down to basement shops and cafes, the other up to a mezzanine bakery. The upper floors of the building have been converted to office use. Old plaster was removed and replaced or if its removal revealed brick walls, these were cleaned and left exposed. Woodwork was refinished or restored where necessary, and except for the addition of graphics, made to look as much as possible like the early office building.

GRAND CENTRAL ON THE PARK, Seattle, Washington. Owners: *Alan Black, Richard White, Ralph Anderson.* Architects: *Ralph Anderson and Partners.* Engineers: *Olsen & Ratti* (structural). Contractor: *Fleming Sorenson Construction Company.*

Grand Central on the Park occupies an important site in the Pioneer Square Historic District, on the corner of the area's principal street, First Avenue, and Main Street which connects directly with Occidental Park and Occidental Mall, two attractive outdoor pedestrian spaces. The park, designed by landscape architects Jones and Jones, was one of the city's contributions to the rehabilitation of the district. Through its arcade concourse, Grand Central on the Park has a strong relation to the Park, since it can be entered either from First Avenue or from the Park, and the dining pavilion of one of its restaurants projects onto the cobbled paving of the park. The old photograph of the building before restoration shows how few changes were needed on the exterior—and how important to the character and quality of the finished building those changes are.

Art Hupy photos

The inviting entrance to this office on one of the upper floors fits into an arched opening in one of the old brick walls exposed during remodelling. Graphics in bright colors enliven the corridor and reduce the apparent height of the ceiling. New windows in a modernized office overlook the park, and the exposed red brick of one wall enriches by color and texture. The arcade at street level serves not only as entrance to office building and shops and cafes but also as concourse between First Avenue and the Park. The handsome iron grille and gate at the Avenue end, old chandeliers and a working fireplace add to the personal scale and character of the arcade.

9

The program called upon architects Robinson & Mills to design a small, modern bookstore off the grand, neo-classic entrance lobby of San Francisco's Museum of Art. Because of the building's landmark character, no external sign was allowed. Identifying graphics were restricted to the overhead, interior curved surface facing the street window. The architects began with a space that had functioned as two adjacent storage rooms. The central column was simply a fact of life. To set up a gentle flow pattern, using the intruding column as a pivot, a curved wall was introduced for book display. The circular theme is continued in the print rack, the sales desk and the portable, plastic-domed display cabinets. To emphasize this easy, uninterrupted flow visually, the designers striped the top of the walls and columns in black and white—a feature that is playfully reflected on the ceiling of silver vinyl. Other finish materials are kept light in color to augment and enliven these colorful, overhead reflections.

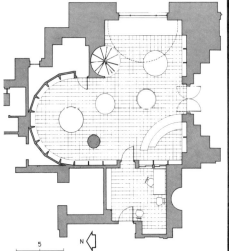

MUSEUM BOOKSTORE, San Francisco Museum of Art. Architects: *Robinson & Mills (Jeffrey L. Teel, project designer)*; mechanical engineer: *Paul E. Rosenthal*; electrical engineers: *Darmsted-Parenti & Associates*; graphic consultants: *Reis & Manwaring*; contractor: *Jacks & Irvine, Inc.*

Morley Baer photos

10

The remodeling of the ground and second floors of this building had as its aim not only renovation of the galleries, but reduction by half of the gallery space on the ground floor (the other half was to be rented). At the same time, the new spaces were not to look as if the operation was smaller in scale than it had been. In addition, the new design had to encourage clients to visit the second-floor showroom. A new semi-circular entry of curved glass lets passersby "feel the inside of the gallery"; a curving ramp (over which part of the second floor was removed for greater height) leads to the stairway to the upper gallery. Stainless steel trim accents the all-white walls.

IRVING GALLERIES, Milwaukee, Wisconsin. Architect: *David Kahler of the office of Fitzhugh Scott.* Contractor: *J. M. Nuetzi, Inc.*

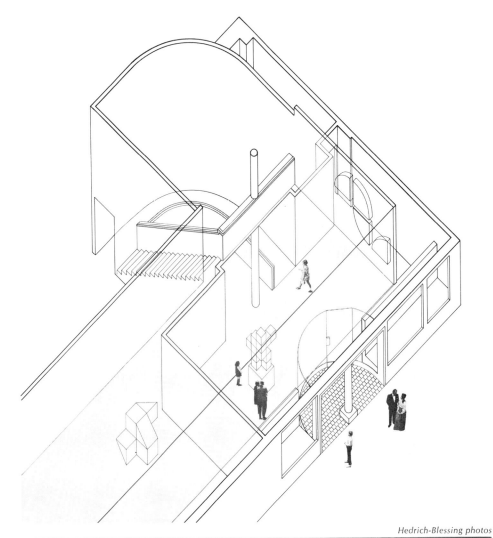

Hedrich-Blessing photos

11

The Lincoln Memorial Bookshop is located in space that formerly served as a "warming room" for important persons on ceremonial occasions. The eight-foot-high space has been turned into a handsome, sophisticated and elegantly simple two-level magnet for tourists looking for souvenirs to remind them of their visit to the monument. All surfaces of the shop are covered with blue carpet, and brilliant points of light both provide the needed illumination and also contrast with the light monumental space outside. A steel platform and open, chrome-railed stair convert the narrow high, presumed unusable space into an inviting and intimately-scaled attraction.

LINCOLN MEMORIAL BOOKSHOP, Washington, D.C. Architect: *Hugh Newell Jacobsen.* Engineer: *Gaza Illis* (mechanical).

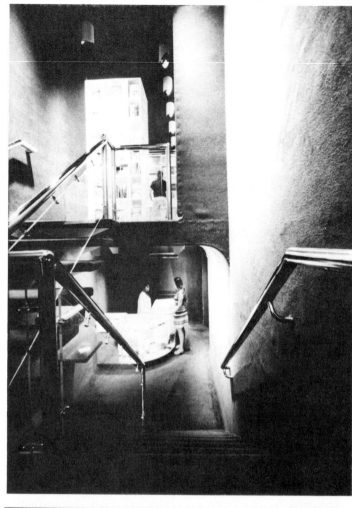

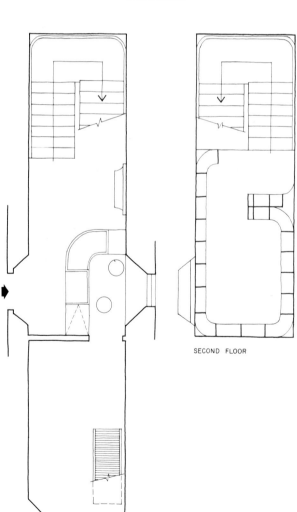

FIRST FLOOR

SECOND FLOOR

12

The Renwick Gallery Museum Shop in Washington, D.C., is located in space previously used for exhibition. Little of that character has been changed, but what changes have been made proclaim the new use, subtly but with strength. Windows on the side of the building toward Blair House have been sealed off for security; the walls have been painted a strong green color and new lighting has been installed. Otherwise, except for refinished floors, the room is as it had been for many years. The display cases, of oak flooring and brass fittings, with bright integral lighting, can be used in a variety of ways, as the difference between plan and photograph shows.

THE RENWICK GALLERY MUSEUM SHOP, Washington, D.C. Architect: *Hugh Newell Jacobsen.* Lighting consultant: *Douglas Baker.*

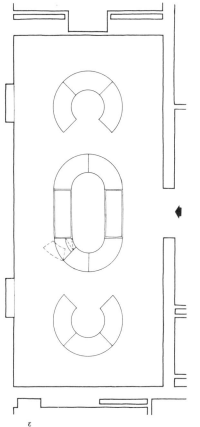

13

Working with a very old existing building and making a minimum of structural changes, the architects utilized brightly-colored reflective surfaces and soft, voluptuous curves to create this high-style, flexible shopping environment. The element used again and again is a cardboard sono-tube, normally employed as a form in pouring concrete columns, but here serving as display case, dressing cubicle and space modulator. The tubes are finished in red, orange and blue lacquer or wrapped in chrome Mylar. Other finish materials include textured plaster, glass, stainless steel and wool carpeting over glazed quarry tile.

The architects were responsible for all design, including graphics, logos, shopping bags and boxes.

ALANDALES MEN'S STORE, Westwood, California. Owner: *Glen Laiken.* Architects: *Zimmerman, Robbin & Associates—project designer: James Stafford.* Engineer: *Norm Epstein* (structural). Graphics: *Roger Kennedy.* Artist: *Theresa Woodward.* Contractor: *Aaron Kommel.* (Aaron Kommel)

Marvin Rand photos

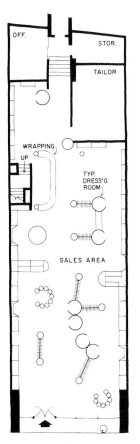

14

With restraint and a limited palette of colors and tones—brown and white—and just a few materials—stainless steel, plastic laminates on counters and cabinets, vinyl covering on walls, terrazzo floors—the architects for this hair styling salon in downtown San Francisco have achieved the distinctive look which their client asked for. Inasmuch as Vidal Sassoon introduced the crisp, classic look to hair styles, he requires that his salons reflect his design sense, and this San Francisco salon, like others in this country and in Europe, is in this vein. He believes, for instance, that hair styling is no mysterious act, and therefore the processes involved should be visible. This salon makes these processes visible not only in the shop but from the street as well, through location of work stations within full view of passersby. There are no screens or partitions; the plan is open and uncluttered. Cupboards and counters are custom designed by the architects and locally made. The only graphics or decoration consist of mounted photographs and, of course, the good looking, stylized logo.

VIDAL SASSOON SALON, San Francisco, California. Architects: *Gordon Bowyer & Partners; Robert H. Hersey, associated architect.* Engineers: *Sexton, Fitzgerald, & Kaplan* (structural); *O'Kelly & Schoenlank* (mechanical). Contractor: *Plant Brothers Corporation.*

**SECOND FLOOR
MEN'S SALON**

Lighting is especially effective, particularly in the women's section on the first floor: track lights are directed toward a baffle, painted white, which bounces it off to the customer and to the counter of each work station. Brown and white, accented by stainless steel, is also used in the men's second floor section.

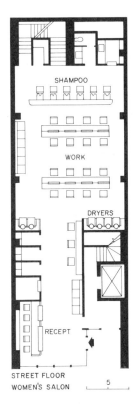

**STREET FLOOR
WOMEN'S SALON**

5

Gerald Ratto photos

15

Transparency—both from the street and within the store itself—is the device used to give this sporting goods shop its magnetic quality. Set into a portion of an old building, once a major department store in downtown San Francisco, the crystalline appearance of the shop contrasts sharply with other stores on the block. A full width, full height glass wall makes up the façade. The discreet identifying sign is carried on a transparent panel which runs across the façade, and large bold lettering on the glass wall, perpendicular to the sign, indicates this as a branch store. "Floating" platforms cut the 24-foot height from lowest to top floor, with a minimum interruption of space, since connecting stairs have transparent balustrades. The main entrance from the street is at the middle level, so customers usually climb no more than one flight, if they climb at all. Complementing the spatial scheme are the inventive and versatile furnishings, designed by the architects, of which the bright red tubular changing booth (below, right), actually a section of concrete form, is an example.

STREETER & QUARLES WEST, San Francisco, California. Architects: *Robert Mittelstadt, Monte S. Bell—Robert Mittelstadt,* project designer. Engineers: *Forell-Chan* (structural); *Mel Cammissa* (electrical). Photo murals: *Lloyd Johnson.*

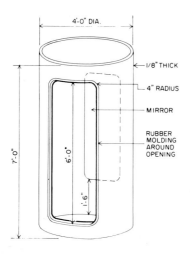

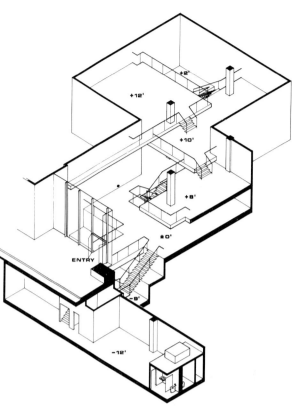

16

Part of a major renovation of United Airlines' four-story building in San Francisco, this showcase ticket office opens across a busy intersection toward Union Square. Architects Arthur Gensler & Associates turned the axis of the ticket lobby on the diagonal to face the square. From this decision, others followed directly. The enclosing glass wall was kept free of the exterior column line and allowed to step in and out, creating a series of small bays and considerable visual interest. The diagonal axis is strongly re-emphasized in the ticket counters, the lighting coffers over the counters and the saw-toothed wall behind.

Bright primary colors and sparkling interior finishes generate enormous excitement. Floors are dark brick, partitions are plasterboard, counters are covered in plastic laminate and columns are clad in polished stainless steel to reduce their bulk and reflect the movement and color within the space. A white-on-white relief, displaying the United Airlines logo along with the principal cities served, forms a spirited and strongly textured end wall.

UNITED AIRLINES TICKET OFFICE, San Francisco, California. Architects: *M. Arthur Gensler & Associates—Don Kennedy, project architect.* Engineers: *Forell-Elsesser-Chan* (structural); *Higash & Associates* (mechanical); *Shinn & Associates* (electrical). Contractor: *Arthur Brothers, Inc.*

Morley Baer photos

Renovation and Remodeling for Community Use

Most cities and many towns have a reservoir of old and obsolescent buildings suitable, by spatial volume and by location, for conversion to use as concert halls, arts centers, cinemas, or other community uses. Whether privately or publicly financed is beside the point, which is that a good old building can provide for a good new use.

Some fortunate cities still have extant movie theaters of the exuberant, romantic Twenties, ebullient Rococo relics of that golden era of the movies. St. Louis, Pittsburgh and Oakland are among such lucky cities. The refurbished buildings, remodeled only to the extent that the needs of their new uses required, again serve the public—as symphony halls—in an elegance which could not otherwise have been afforded today.

Simpler, more mundane buildings, like the carriage house that became a community arts center, or the adjacent warehouses that were turned into three art film theaters, also have excellent possibilities of new, and needed, use in the field of public entertainment. Even though such complete change of use as turning a carriage house into a place of public assembly may entail much ingenuity in meeting code requirements, such problems can be successfully overcome, as the converted structures in this chapter clearly show. These buildings, like other rehabilitated and renovated buildings, have been important influences in the revitalizing of the neighborhoods in which they are located.

1

When Loew's Penn theater closed its doors in 1964, after providing film and vaudeville entertainment for 37 years, demolition seemed inevitable. After all, on all sides of the Golden Triangle, old structures were being pulled down and replaced by shiny metal-skinned towers. But circumstances held a far different fate for the building.

On September 10, 1971, the Penn theater became the Heinz Hall for the Performing Arts. Plans to renovate the building for its new use began in 1968 after test concerts in the theater (see marquee, above) proved that not only did the room work well for symphonic music but that Pittsburghers were very willing to come downtown for concerts. Henry J. Heinz II, through the Howard Heinz Endowment, agreed to purchase the building and to substantially pay for the cost of rehabilitating it— approximately ten million dollars to date. The 2,730-seat hall now serves not only the renowned Pittsburgh Symphony but the Pittsburgh Opera, the Civic Light Opera, the Pittsburgh Ballet and the Youth Symphony as well.

Although the neo-Baroque opulence of the old movie palace yet remains, the technical requirements necessary for revamping the building to its new use have been achieved economically and unobtrusively. In addition to restoring the Grand Foyer, the Grand Lobby and the hall itself to a tasteful reflection of the late twenties, the architects and their many consultants revised circulation patterns thoroughly with a new lobby (right center), intermission lounges and staircase, (right, bottom), provided three floors of offices for the various performing groups, added a wing behind the stage containing enlarged backstage space and other support facilities, and finally—under the direction of Dr. Heinrich Keilholz of Salzburg, Austria—added a large acoustical reflector above the proscenium and other refinements for optimal sound delivery in a multi-purpose hall.

Symphony, ballet, and especially opera performances, as opposed to moviegoing, require spacious and comfortable rooms in which to relax and greet friends during intermissions. The mezzanine remodeling shows two major additions for that purpose. A new horseshoe staircase from the main floor to the mezzanine brings the audience to a new lounge and to the Grand Foyer, formerly a space open to the main floor but now bridged at the mezzanine level to provide intermission space. Where once the marquee glittered, a four-story window reveals the Grand Lobby to evening passersby, (right). The newly-built ticket lobby is en-

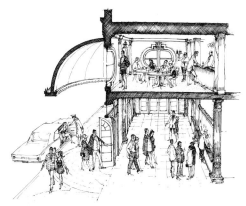

tered by five doorways under copper-sheathed cupolas. The bulb-lined cupolas serve not only to shelter the entrances, but to screen the view of those in the lounge from flashing neon signs on the shops across the street (section above).

A six-story addition behind the existing building spans an important city utility right-of-way in order to permit a stage twice as deep as before. Two two-story rehearsal rooms, dressing rooms, practice rooms, instrument storage, a music library, performers' entrance and other circulation space is included in a compact new building.

The most intriguing technical aspect of concert hall design is, of course, the acoustical one. Here, Dr. Keilholz, who has an impressive list of accomplishments, including the final and successful work at New York's Philharmonic Hall, has used the classic technique of reflection from solid, hard surfaces to reinforce the energy transmitted to the listener by the orchestra or singer. A movable but heavily-built enclosure around the orchestra combined with the reflector, overpage, and panels floated above the players produces clear but lively sound images for a variety of performance requirements. In addition to these elements, Dr. Keilholz has specified an electro-acoustical system that permits sound reinforcement of certain productions, although not symphony or opera music.

HEINZ HALL OF THE PERFORMING ARTS, Pittsburgh, Pennsylvania. Architects: *Stotz, Hess, MacLachlan and Fosner.* Engineers: *George Levinson* (structural); *Meucci Engineering, Inc.* (mechanical); *Hornfeck Engineering, Inc.* (electrical). Consultants: *Dr. Heinrich Keilholz* (acoustical and stage technique); *Verner S. Purcell* (interior design). General contractor: *Melton-Stuart Company.*

Although the only changes in the audience portion of Heinz Hall (right) are new seats and a considerably restrained redecorating of walls and ceilings, the acoustical elements added to make it a first-rate symphony hall are quite evident. The large reflector above the proscenium (shown left) under construction with the circular frames for the twelve chandeliers is made of hard plaster on a steel frame. The orchestra enclosure is stressed seven-ply ¾-inch plywood sheets in movable steel frames that permit the enclosure depth to vary more than 15 feet. One of the two-story rehearsal rooms in the new wing (left bottom) has plywood baffles on walls and ceilings. The plans and sections (below) show that most of the changes in the renovation took place in the lobby and backstage areas of the building. Seating capacity was reduced by 700 seats because of increased seat spacing and removal of some seats in the uppermost balcony.

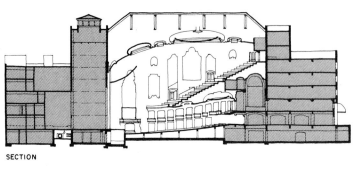

SECTION

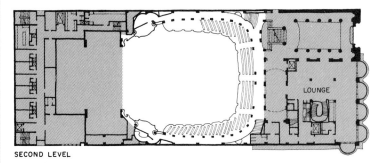

SECOND LEVEL

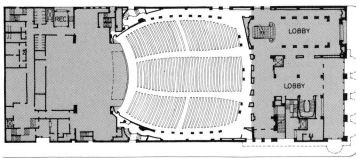

FIRST LEVEL

When Stanley Goodman and others interested in the St. Louis Symphony began seeking a new and permanent home for their orchestra, the usual options were examined. New construction of a suitable concert house (estimated cost $15-20 million) was a possibility, of course, but when the old St. Louis movie theater (at top) became available, its virtues were almost irresistible. It had been built in the twenties by architects Rapp and Rapp of Chicago, who had lavished on the building a high level of decoration and detail even for that period of decorative richness. Preliminary tests indicated that the acoustics were good. The structure was sound and required few structural alterations for conversion to symphonic use. Work on the project commenced immediately.

The design goal was to create an excellent modern concert facility with the warmth and opulence of the old Baroque houses of Europe. Lighting designer David Mintz filled out the spindly chandeliers over the grand foyer, carefully replicating their crystal details but increasing their bulk considerably. Additional downlighting was added to the ceiling which was then painted to brighten the space and selectively simplify the detail. Both in the foyer and in the house, the designers simplified where they could by removing unwanted detail and retaining what was best.

The house itself was fitted with new seats, repainted off-white, regilded and relamped. Mintz removed two-thirds of the bulbs (which were red, white and blue) in the magnificent ceiling dome (photo left) and added downlights in a pattern that reinforced the ceiling geometry. Uplighting is provided by wall fixtures, some of them concealed, that illuminate the ceiling and reveal its forms and details without disturbing the dome's gentle glow.

What seems most striking about the completed project is the skill with which the modifications proceeded. The process of selective subtraction has resulted in a modern concert hall with superb acoustics but without any visible sacrifice of elegance or those magical, fantasy qualities to which concertgoers still respond most warmly.

POWELL HALL, St. Louis, Missouri. Architect: *Angelo Corrubia*. Theater consultant: *Ben Schlanger*. Engineers: *Cyril Harris* (acoustical); *Ken Balk and Associates* (structural); *Ross and Baruzzini* (mechanical). Interiors: *Clark Davis, William Bernoudy*. Lighting: *David Mintz with Lewis Smith*. Contractor: *Rallo Construction Company*.

3

The rehabilitation of carriage houses, in those communities lucky enough to have them, for residential use began as soon as the automobile replaced the horse-drawn carriage. As in most residential work, the architectural and legal problems are relatively simple. But when the carriage house is converted to public use, as was this one at the Newark Community Center of the Arts, the designer must deal with code requirements as stringent as those for new construction of the same type. Thus, a building of 2,000 square feet must accommodate two means of egress, provide adequate toilets, and meet the same codes as larger structures.

With a limited budget and area in which to work, the architects provided rehearsal and performance space for music and dance which works well and admirably captures the spirit of the school. Mrs. David Lass and Saunders Davis, music teachers in the Newark school system, established the Center in January, 1968. Enrollment grew so rapidly that new quarters were needed within six months. Grants from two foundations enabled the school to move into a large house in a once well-to-do Newark neigh-

borhood. Soon afterwards the architects began the conversion of the carriage house behind.

Although the roof and some of the masonry of the existing building had to be replaced, the 20-foot-wide shell dictated the proportions of the revised design. The alley façade (top of the plan, opposite page) remains as it was with all new construction toward the house (which now contains offices and music rehearsal rooms). Performance-goers pass through the house into a courtyard, which will be developed as an outdoor theater, across which they see the sprightly elevation at left. A split-level entrance leads down to toilets and mirrored rehearsal room with an elegant two-position barre and new hardwood floor. The stairs bring audiences up directly into a large room divided diagonally into stage and seating areas. Faced with a 2:5 plan proportion, the architects felt that the diagonal stage permitted the width necessary for dance movement, as a standard stage across one end would not, while not spreading the audience the entire length of the space. A new roof structure echoes and reinforces the stage angle while a clerestory over the audience increases the sense of enclosure about the stage. Performers can come onto the stage from a ramp leading to the lower floor or can enter from an alcove over the lobby. An adjustable stage lighting system adds a glamorous note.

NEWARK COMMUNITY CENTER OF THE ARTS, Newark, New Jersey. Architects: *Hardy, Holzman and Pfeiffer Associates.* General contractor: *Verfield Construction Company, Inc.*

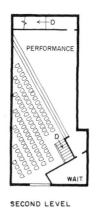

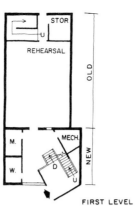

PERFORMANCE

WAIT

SECOND LEVEL

STOR

REHEARSAL

M.

W.

MECH.

OLD

NEW

FIRST LEVEL

4

This conversion of one and a half floors of a former automobile sales agency into three intimate theaters is remarkably handsome and workable especially since the building's upper (garage) floors provide essential parking space. The theaters range in size from 130 to 170 seats, and are served by one lobby with one employee who doubles as both ticket-seller and concessionaire. A short flight of steps from the lobby leads to the mezzanine off which the theaters are entered. Above the theaters are the restrooms and projection room, reached by the dramatic stairway painted bright red. Mirrored ceilings add to the apparent size of the mezzanine which serves as a waiting area.

CERBERUS THEATERS, Washington, D.C. Architects: *Bull Field Volkmann Stockwell—John Louis Field, partner-in-charge*. Associated architects: *Wilkes & Faulkner*. Graphics: *Reis and Mainwaring*. Contractor: *Coleman & Wood*.

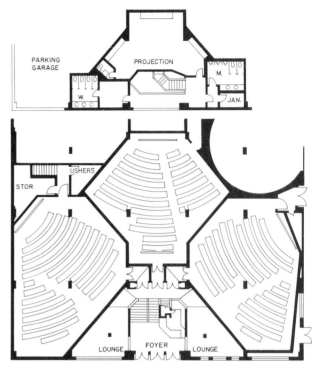

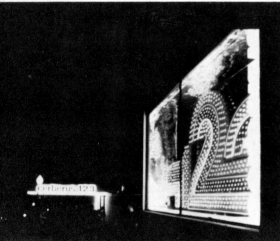

Norman McGrath photos

Entering the lobby and waiting areas of the Cerberus Theaters invites a complete change in pace—even, as the architects say, a "suspension of the familiar habits of space." The sophisticated and essentially simple interiors —dark grey walls with accents of bright color and mirror ceiling brilliantly reflecting the bare electric bulbs—make a particularly effective introduction to the world of the art film. Advance ticket sales reduce the need for a large ticketing lobby, and a staggered schedule of film showings makes a large waiting area unnecessary. The theater's exterior, a radical but again simple transformation from its former appearance, meets ingeniously the Georgetown restriction against theater signs: the architects and their graphics consultants designed a 60-foot-long light mural for the old auto display windows which, by its color and changing design, is a traffic-stopper. Incandescent and neon lighting in the three bands of color is multiplied by the mirror-lining of the window box. The light mural incorporates the theater name and the billboard for the three theaters.

5

These three theaters do indeed make up a cinema center, as their name suggests. Located in two former warehouses, they are reached by a skylighted arcade off which also open a restaurant and a shop. This combination of commercial facilities is warranted by the location of the buildings: they are in a rapidly developing tourist section of Oakland, adjacent to highly successful Jack London Square. The arcade provides waiting area for patrons and is wide enough to allow the traffic flow in both directions. It also takes care of the problem of joining usefully the two buildings, one of which originally was entered from a side street. In addition to the arcade, these theaters also have a large lobby.

CINEMA THREE CENTER, Oakland, California. Architects: *Bull Field Volkmann Stockwell—John Louis Field, partner-in-charge.* Structural engineers: *GFDS Engineers.* Acoustical consultants: *Fitzroy/Dobbs.* Interior design: *Bull Field Volkmann Stockwell.* Graphics: *BFVS.* Contractor: *Strauss Construction Company, Inc.*

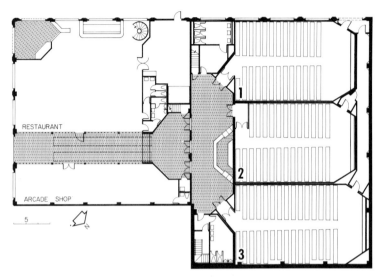

Jim Cheng photos

6

One of the problems of the downtown movie theater is parking space: you can't get patrons unless they can leave their cars. This double theater, located in the street level retail rental space of a Connecticut Avenue office building in Washington, D.C., uses the building's below-grade parking garage in its off-hours—nights and Sundays, the theaters' hours of operation. The colorful ceramic tile wall mosaic, designed by the architects, attracts attention and also acts as a sign board, a happy compromise which the city's restrictions on signs in this area made necessary. The marquis, permitted by code, is a good-looking landmark. One theater seats 153, the other, 180; one lobby serves both. Multiple mirrors make possible film projection from a single booth.

JANUS 1 & 2 THEATERS, Washington, D.C. Architect: *John Louis Field*. Associate architect: *Hugh Newell Jacobsen*. Contractor: *Tuckman-Barbee Construction, Inc.*

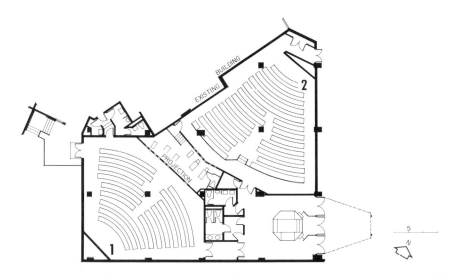

Rehabilitation and Renovation for Reuse

Architectural character may be, however, the strongest determinant of the value of renovating and reusing an old building: who could envision, for instance, building today the eclectic, yet exceptionally handsome, Williston Library at Mount Holyoke College, or the solid classic dignity of Welles Bosworth's MIT library? We would not duplicate them if we could, yet each in its own way justifies, by its character, renovation and reuse, and so preserves for new generations a quality and an architectural character not possible today.

Whether a building is to be, after its modernization, a kind of charming anachronism (though fully functional) like the Levi Strauss plant in San Francisco, or whether it is to take on contemporary overtones—because it seeks thereby to attract patrons—as does the Clinton Youth and Family Center in New York City, depends on the virtues (or faults) of the original building. The more respectful the changes, the more valued the old building will be. A lot will also depend on the owner's view of the economics of the situation: it makes excellent sense to retain a well-built old building whose use has not been outlived even though its interior condition (though usually not its exterior) has become obsolete.

Vano, Wells, Fagliano photos

1

Soon after the savage fire of 1906, Levi Strauss & Company (makers of the well-known clothing line) began construction of a large manufacturing plant in downtown San Francisco. The structure was a three-story wood frame box of pleasant proportions but no particular architectural distinction. Since original construction, both the building and the neighborhood had gradually deteriorated.

In renovating this building, architect Howard Friedman's somewhat whimsical approach was to create "a sort of Disneyland Western Hotel look—in keeping with Levi's original cowboy image." Four stair towers were added at the building's corners to meet the city's standards for required exits. The porch was constructed for period style and to provide a place for employees and public to relax. A playground for public use was added as a commitment to the neighborhood. The interior planning, by contrast, is serious in intent and reflects 1971 corporate functions. The heavy wood structure—posts, trusses and plank floors—was retained and highlighted with color. Functions within the building have been redistributed. A new sculptural light court, new partitioning, lighting and mechanical equipment complete this spirited and timely renovation.

LEVI STRAUSS & COMPANY, San Francisco, California. Architects: *Howard A. Friedman & Associates.* Engineers: *Kasin, Guttman and Associates* (mechanical). General contractor: *Maloney & O'Hare.*

Renovation of this building has lent impetus to a drive toward upgrading the appearance of the whole neighborhood. The sharing of playground equipment with neighborhood children has met with warm affirmative response. After almost a year of use in an area characterized in the past by widespread vandalism, not one pane of glass or lighting fixture has needed replacement.

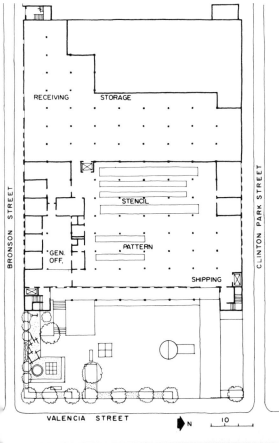

2

Mount Sinai Hospital in New York City has been in a continuous state of remodeling for the last two decades, a condition any growing hospital today finds inevitable. One firm—Kahn and Jacobs—has performed most of this work, adding several entirely new buildings, and remodeling a campus of 26 older structures varying in age from 9 to 67 years.

The building shown here is a conversion of old open-ward nursing units (see photo, opposite) to semi-private acute patient rooms that are fully serviced with central air conditioning, toilets in each patient's room, and piped oxygen and vacuum systems overhead.

The key to remodeling was the quality of the old building itself. It was originally designed as an open-ward center in 1900 by Arnold W. Brunner, a New York City architect, and it has a handsome neo-renaissance facade that has been retained, as the picture at the right shows. It was also built with a sound masonry and steel structural system, vaulted flooring (middle photo, right) and a substantial floor-to-floor height —17 feet, 10 inches. Before air conditioning, a high ceiling was a common mode for aiding human comfort. Because of the ceiling height, Kahn and Jacobs were able to remodel in stages, and provide the remodeled nursing units with a modern concept in hospital planning: that is, the flexibility of "interstitial spaces" for the housing of mechanical systems immediately above and below the working floor levels.

Above is the façade of the old open-ward unit which has been allowed to remain intact, with some changes in elevation and circulation at the ground level. Before, during, and after stages of reconstruction are shown from top to bottom in the series of three photographs at the right, and the section, far right, illustrates construction of the interstitial mechanical spaces.

The alteration was executed in stages so that a typical floor could be reconstructed while all the rest of the floors were in use, as in the large section, far right. The phasing went something like this: all vertical piping was brought to the underside of the third floor (for instance) while that floor was still occupied. Patients were then relocated from the third floor, and existing construction was demolished and removed. A permanent full-floor catwalk was then constructed ten feet above the floor, and all lateral distribution piping and other mechanical components were installed from the catwalk. Finally, new partitions and finishes were added to the third floor below the catwalk and the floor was re-occupied by patients. Then the fourth floor was evacuated and demolished, beginning the process again.

This rebuilding provided "as new" facilities at a construction cost of under $16,000.00 per bed. It would have been impossible to accomplish had the original building been removed, or had it been originally constructed on a smaller bay module with less ceiling height. The investigations to determine what old construction should be saved, and how to best use that old construction for new facilities, is largely up to the architects, and of course this kind of creative rehabilitation work is an important part of many large architectural offices today.

MOUNT SINAI MEDICAL CENTER REMODELING, New York City. Architects: *Kahn and Jacobs—Robert W. Hegardt, project architect.* Engineers: *Chester & Chester* (structural); *Jansen & Rogan* (mechanical). Interiors: *K & J Designs.* Project coordinator for Mt. Sinai: *Rosemary Tetrault.* Contractors: *D.M.&L. Construction.*

Jay Hoops photos

3

St. Vincent's Monastery outside Pittsburgh is a complex of buildings, the earliest of which was constructed about 125 years ago. The various buildings are stylistically divergent but each is fashioned of handmade brick by masons who obviously took special delight in the work of their hands.

When fire gutted many of the buildings a decade ago, Tasso Katselas was commissioned to prepare a new master plan—or "master concept" as he prefers to describe it—that envisioned a series of changes extensive in scope and duration. The newer work—extensive in itself—included a new main entrance to the administrative wing (photo left). This required removing an old warehouse and relocating the nuns' quarters to a new portion of the campus-like plan. To create a new reception area, Katselas removed the floor of one space (photo right), but left in place the existing system of wood beams notched to receive floor joists. While visiting is somewhat restricted, this space has become a hub of activities and the monastery staff wonders how it got along for a century without such a space.

In the course of removing old materials and finishes, Katselas has found a variety of old spaces of unusual interest. An old milk cellar, for instance, was uncovered adjacent to the reception area shown at right and it was subsequently converted into a meditation and conference space.

Under the monastery, and connecting many of its buildings, Katselas found a labyrinthine series of interconnected tunnels, some of them for access to mechanical services, but others that included beautifully built spaces with vaulted stone ceilings. These will be retained and renovated to provide covered (albeit underground) circulation between the buildings.

While St. Vincent's represents renovation at an unusually large scale, Katselas has been careful to retain much of what was good and has resisted the temptation to replace indiscriminately those elements that give St. Vincent's and its brotherhood a sense of continuity and order.

RENOVATION OF ST. VINCENT'S MONASTERY, Latrobe, Pennsylvania. Architect: *Tasso Katselas.* Engineers: *R. M. Gensert and Associates* (structural); *Environment Inc.* (mechanical/electrical). Landscape consultant: *Joseph Hajains.* Contractors: *Pivarnik Brothers and Dill Construction Company.*

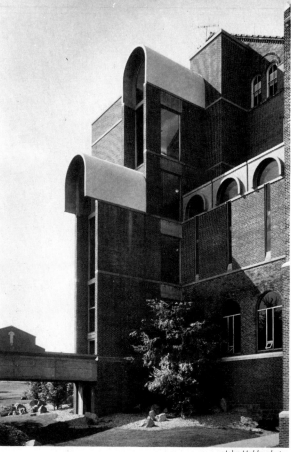

John Hobbs photos

Wayne Soverns Jr. photos except as noted

4

J. Ph. Charbonnier

The Massachusetts Institute of Technology dome is an imposing landmark, as seen from the principal entrance façade (below). Designed by Welles Bosworth in 1916 as part of his scheme for the neo-classic East Campus, it has long been the crown of the reading room of MIT's engineering library.

The library interior has now been remodeled by Walter Netsch of SOM. Netsch has successfully juxtaposed his own geometry, based upon an intricate system of intersecting diagonals, with the classic form of the dome's interior. By this means, he has produced eight clearly articulated reading areas plus an additional study space at the center. The outer ring of the dome has been remodeled to more efficiently continue its

Courtesy MIT

original function of housing stacks, research areas and administrative spaces, and to accommodate the new computer hardware developed as part of MIT's so-called Project Intrex. The latter is a new form of information transfer designed to handle the growing collection.

The library as a whole has been conceived as a flexible unit. The division between its traditional library functions—browsing, study and research—and its sophisticated, computerized information retrieval system has deliberately been made imperceptible.

For many years the interior of the MIT dome was
hidden by a suspended luminous ceiling of corrugated
translucent plastic lit by fluorescents. A product
of an era noted for destructive remodeling in the
name of function, this ceiling was hung just below
the column capitals. In addition to ruining the
room as a space (opposite page far left), it created
a harsh and unpleasant glare. Netsch's first decision
was to remove the suspended ceiling and expose the
dome once more. This called for extensive restoration
of the dome and its moldings. The oculus, formerly
translucent, was made opaque and powerful lights
were placed around its perimeter as part of a
cross-lighting system designed to emphasize the
shape of the dome. The pole-supported lighting
fixtures also illuminate the dome transforming
it into a reflecting surface. These light trees
illuminate the working surfaces as well. The
carrel lighting, highlighting of the publication
racks and supplementary local lighting was carefully
studied. Walls, columns and the dome ceiling were
painted white to further brighten the room.

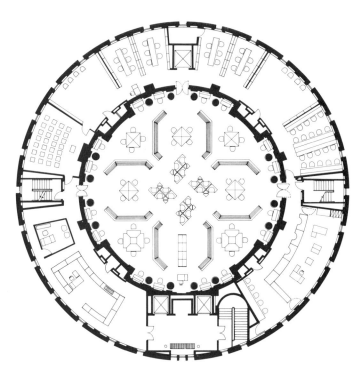

FIFTH FLOOR

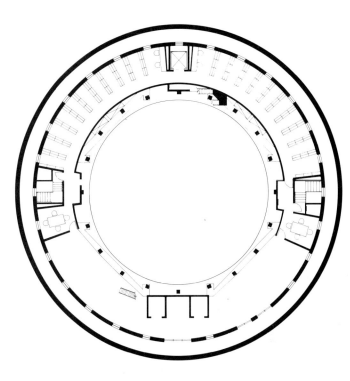

EIGHTH FLOOR

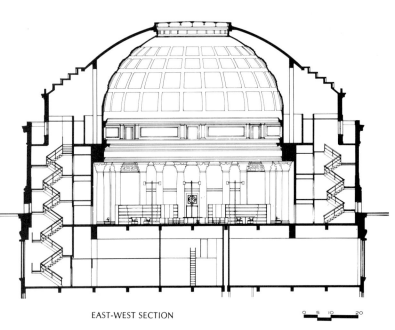

EAST-WEST SECTION

0 5 10   20

The unyielding and unwieldy total geometry of the dome gave Netsch more repetitious concentric circles and truncated pie-shapes to work with than he would have chosen, and there were other problems. The library had to be open and in operation during the entire reconstruction project; the dome, though beautiful, possesses construction oddities that could not be ignored, altered or circumvented; and the remodeling budget was limited. Netsch had to achieve his effects by essentially non-structural means—furniture design and placement, redesigned lighting and acoustics, selection of sculpture, plants and color.

The plan concentrates two major working areas for greater user efficiency. Nearly all requirements for searching or browsing are on the fifth floor at the entrance level. Here, in addition to circulation and reference services, are facilities for literature search, computer-controlled literature search, current journals, and individual study spaces at carrels, tables or in lounge chairs. Staff members' offices and work areas are chiefly on the fourth floor—out of the sight and sound of users.

THE JAMES MADISON BARKER ENGINEERING LIBRARY, Massachusetts Institute of Technology, Cambridge, Massachusetts. Architects for the interiors: *Skidmore, Owings & Merrill —Walter Netsch, partner in charge.* Consultants: *Dr. Carl Overage and Charles Stevens* (Project Intrex staff); *MIT Electronic Systems Laboratory* (hardware development); *Bolt, Beranek and Newman* (acoustics); *William Lam* (lighting). General contractor: *Fuller Construction Company.*

From the beginning, the library was a hard, reverberant space. Originally the dome itself was blamed for the poor acoustics and this belief helped justify the installation of the suspended luminous ceiling which Netsch removed. At the time of the current remodeling, however, Bolt, Beranek and Newman, the acoustical consultants, persuaded MIT that the hard plaster walls and terrazzo floor were the cause of the difficulty. Excessive noise and echo have now been absorbed by the use of carpet on the backs of the freestanding periodical racks (opposite page top, left) as well as on the floor. Although the acousticians did not think it necessary, sound absorbent panels were placed within the smallest rectangle of each of the dome coffers. The chairs (below) were designed by Vasarely. The suspended, mobile, cast-aluminum sculpture (below and opposite page) is by Robert Engman. It was donated to MIT by art collector Netsch. Both chairs and mobile are combinations of circles and are thus appropriate forms for a domed room.

5

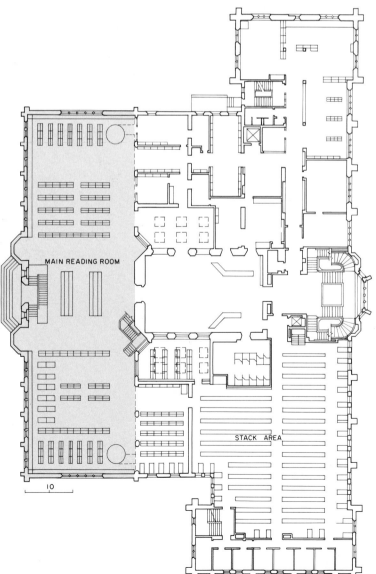

The original chandeliers (above) have been reworked (as shown at right), and additional high-intensity concealed source lighting was added, vastly improving study conditions in the main reading room. The number of seating spaces was reduced in this room and additional shelving was installed instead. Throughout the library as a whole, however, there has been an increase in formal and informal study facilities.

MAIN READING ROOM

STACK AREA

10

From the exterior it is difficult to discern any change to this highly visible library on Mt. Holyoke's old campus, but its interior has been significantly altered to respond to today's needs. Its usefulness has been extended to the year 2000 and possibly beyond, all at a cost quite lower than would have been required by a new building or a major addition.

The original building was constructed in 1905, using the bricks saved from a previous library structure that had stood on the site from 1870 to 1904. The first renovation was in 1936 when a new tower, stack area and office and classroom wing were added.

The program for the most recent remodel-ing called for an increase in book capacity from 300,000 to 500,000 volumes and provisions for an increase in readers from 400 to 600. Extensive visual aid facilities were to be added, plus more classrooms, support facilities and study/offices.

After analyzing the program and surveying the existing building, the architects decided that a major addition was not necessary and that a good workable solution could be found within the perimeter of the existing building. Two lightwells were enclosed in the remodeling and now contain dramatically sky-lit spaces for the card catalog and the reserve collection. The original central bookstack core was converted into the entrance foyer including the control desk and the periodical reading area.

The original ornate Collegiate Gothic main reading room (above) was enhanced by the removal of the heavy old furniture and glaring desk lamps that can be seen in the old photograph (opposite page, top). The general illumination has been increased.

WILLISTON LIBRARY RENOVATION, Mount Holyoke College, South Hadley, Massachusetts. Architects: *Hugh Stubbins and Associates, Inc.—project director: Norman Patterson.* Engineers: *LeMessurier Associates, Inc.* (structural); *Greenleaf Associates* (mechanical/electrical). Contractor: *Fontaine Bros.*

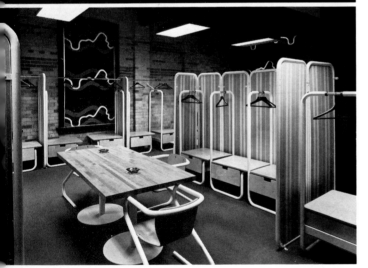

6

The owner of two four-story brick buildings and an adjoining vacant lot commissioned the architects to design a squash club using the existing structures for lounge, locker and restaurant space, then integrating these with a new building containing squash courts constructed on the vacant lot.

The main entry is at the first floor of the new structure and gives access to the 400-seat viewing gallery that overlooks two exhibition courts which are fitted with large, back-wall viewing panels. There are two additional floors of courts on levels 2 and 3 above and these include 15 American singles courts, one English singles court (dimensionally different) and one doubles court. Connected to these playing facilities, but occupying renovated space in the existing structures, are a restaurant (with separate entrance), lockers, lounge spaces and other support facilities (see plans).

The program was unusual and its requirement for blending old and new into a coherent unity was a challenge the architects gladly assumed. The result is an interior that is not only functionally efficient but visibly unified—this in spite of the disparate elements the architects began with and in spite of the radically different requirements placed on each kind of space by the program itself. The interiors, strictly functional, achieve an even level of design concern throughout and seem to convey quite clearly that fun and physical exertion are elements that can be contained and given suitable design expression.

TORONTO SQUASH CLUB, Toronto, Canada. Architects: *Neish, Owen, Rowland & Roy—William J. Neish, partner-in-charge; Peter Manson-Smith, project designer.* Contractor: *Camston Ltd.*

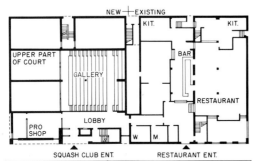

FIRST FLOOR

SECOND FLOOR

7

Just over a year ago, the Yale Club of New York renewed its land lease, extended membership privileges to women and embarked on a program of upgrading its physical facilities. The present building, designed in 1914 by James Gamble Rogers, includes 22 floors of varied club use, much of it in gradually deteriorating condition. Platner's task was to solve certain functional problems in the main lobby, to dress the space up, but to leave its dignified and classically conservative character undisturbed.

Much of the period architecture is new and replaces similar, but deteriorating, construction. All counters, furniture, and lighting is new—almost all of it designed by the architect. Enameled wood, leather and polished brass are the principal materials of renovation.

The architect's determination to care for the symbols and appurtenances of the past seems especially praiseworthy and the skill and sympathy with which he has introduced the present—when necessary—should not go without notice.

YALE CLUB OF NEW YORK, New York City. Architects: *Warren Platner Associates—Mark Mogeridge, Piers Ford, Paul Sargent, associates on this project.* Engineers: *Arthur Edwards* (mechanical and electrical). Contractor: *S. Di Giacomo & Sons, Inc.*

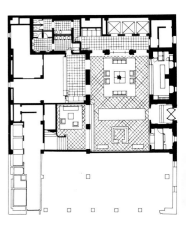

Norman McGrath photos

8

This 77-year-old structure, located on Manhattan's Lower East Side, has long been the headquarters of the Educational Alliance — a settlement house that sprang up before the turn of the century to serve the educational needs of a Jewish immigrant community. As the ethnic character of the community gradually expanded to include other minorities, the Alliance's goals and services have broadened in response. Because its roots are so deep in the community, the Alliance decided to renovate rather than seek quarters at a new location.

In planning the renovation, architect David Specter strove to preserve the building's exterior esthetic while bringing its functional standards up to current levels of acceptability. On the three floors now renovated, many spaces have been reorganized and finish surfaces are largely new. Halls and stairwells are color-saturated with supergraphics that convey information and lend visual enrichment in powerful doses. Throughout the building, Specter has used large photomurals, culled from various archives, that catch the color and flavor of community life at the turn of the century. The photos also serve as a constant reminder of long years of dedicated and uninterrupted service.

DAVID SARNOFF BUILDING OF THE EDUCATIONAL ALLIANCE, New York City, New York. Architect: *David Kenneth Specter.* Engineers: *Wayman C. Wing* (structural); *Flack & Kurtz* (mechanical). Graphics consultant: *Denison Cash Stockman.* Contractor: *Koren-Diresta Company.*

9

Van Brody photos

At least one building among the deteriorating tenement façades of West 54th Street in Manhattan is bright and inviting—as city life and its institutions can be. It is the Clinton Youth and Family Center, once the Seventh District Police Court building. The painted metal doors, windows and new intake pipes for air conditioning make vigorous images for the future, and have at the same time been fitted within the orderly stonework of the past; they seem to say that we need not insist on historically accurate restorations to provide a necessary feeling of continuity with our roots, nor do we need to level old architecture to make cities better. The Youth and Family Center is operated by the YMCA of Greater New York and the Rotary Club of New York, and the majority of the renovation costs were paid for by the Astor Foundation, which has funded several other buildings of worth in New York ghetto areas.

Inside, the old six-story structure built at the beginning of this century has been transformed by brightly painted walls, movable/storable furniture, and plenty of irreverent writing on the walls. The surprisingly appropriate flowing spaces house noisy children and under-financed neighborhood health programs as well as they once housed the solemn, not-too-happy processes of criminal justice. By removing several full-height brick walls erected during previous remodelings, the vaulted solemnity of the old main entrance lobby (top, right) was reclaimed. But elsewhere on the ground floor, in the new lounge and the entrance foyer to the elevators (right and following page), color rather than space has been added. The old wall planes, moldings and right angles have been properly violated by paint in diagonal stripes and overlapping circles, yet the sense of old architecture conserved still remains. This large ground floor space is a kind of "mixing valve" where all of the diverse groups coming in and out of the center each day are brought together.

The center can be understood as having its large-group "mixer" spaces—including the gymnasium—on the lower floors, the park in back, and the progressively smaller and more private-use spaces on the upper floors. The central staircase that connects them all is a finely scaled circular shaft (see isometric, following page) filled with open wrought iron lattice work and skylighted at the top. The center of the shaft used to be occupied by an elevator—the only one in the original court—that unfortunately had to be removed. The old main courtroom is now the gymnasium, with a new maple floor and with bouncing balls and the arc of their travel painted boldly on the brick walls. The coffered ceiling of the courtroom provided excellent recesses for new lighting fixtures, and a classical portico that was a feature of the courtroom has been allowed to remain, now framing a basketball backboard. A second, low-ceilinged courtroom occupied what is now the fourth and fifth floors, but there was no need for a second large space. So, it has been divided into seminar rooms and offices (see isometric, top, page 136) and most of the new partitions on this floor are surfaced with hardboard and left unpainted. These fourth and fifth floors have wall-to-wall carpeting throughout, and they are—not surprisingly—among the most popular for smaller meetings and games.

The renovation commission was received by the architects in 1968, and the project was complete in 1970; it took one year to prepare contract documents and about 18 months for construction. The original contract called for about $400,000 in work, but the cost of the project rose to almost $1 million through change-order additions during construction, as the fundraising drives became more successful and additional money became available for additional work.

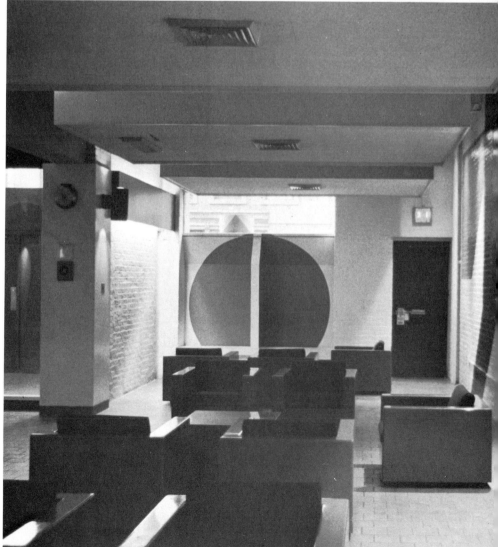

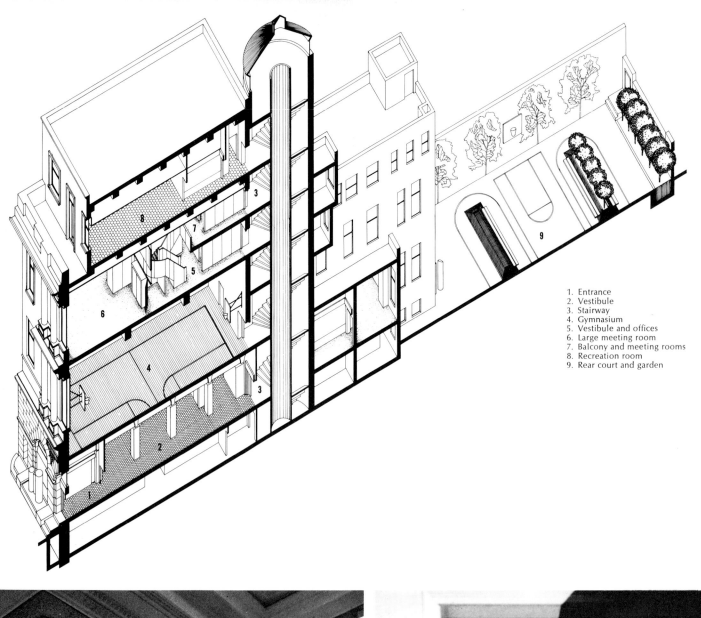

1. Entrance
2. Vestibule
3. Stairway
4. Gymnasium
5. Vestibule and offices
6. Large meeting room
7. Balcony and meeting rooms
8. Recreation room
9. Rear court and garden

The large meeting room on the fourth floor (right) exhibits the graphic skill and color that makes the center as a whole so successful. The three-dimensionality of the windows is painted on, not real, but it is almost better this way. The stair to the fifth-floor mezzanine (below) shows how the unpainted hardboard is used in conjunction with the red carpet, to achieve a remarkable feeling of richness with inexpensive, wear-resistant surfaces. The rear garden (below, right) was once the site of one of the most decrepit jails in Manhattan, torn down in the course of this remodeling at a cost of $90,000. Now the real trees are beginning to grow there, to complement the painted trees on the walls.

- -

CLINTON YOUTH AND FAMILY CENTER, New York City. Architects: *James Stewart Polshek and Associates, and Walfredo Toscanini—J.S. Polshek, project architect.* Graphic design: *James Stewart Polshek and Associates—David Bliss, project designer.* Engineers: *Benjamin & Zicherman Associates.* General contractor: *Dember Construction Corporation.*

Stan Menscher photo

Kozti

Kozti

Theodore Prudon

Julius Shulman

Theodore Prudon

10

Just as with other building types, recycling of existing hotels—or buildings originally designed for other uses into hotels—makes increasing good sense. Sharing the obvious savings on construction costs found in other types of reuse, older structures can forcefully conjure the images of grandeur that constantly elude the hosteler attempting to create "period" atmosphere anew. At the right, is an example of a hotel owned by an independent operator catering to a highly specialized market of the "fashionable" and the affluent. But large corporations are not missing the point—and Holiday Inn and Hyatt corporations are among the more surprising of those currently engaged in projects reusing older structures. Holiday Inn is converting a group of houses in Bruges, Belgium into a hotel; according to one authority, previous attempts to provide American-style motels had been a failure. Hyatt has incorporated an 18th-century house into its hotel in Charleston, South Carolina. The Sonesta Hotel in Amsterdam is to use a 17th-century church as its conference center (Sonesta hotels occupy many recycled buildings.)

Hilton International has recently announced the conversion and extension of a monastery and church tower, dating from the Middle Ages, into a new hotel in Budapest (top two photos). Located in an historic district and across the street from the traditional crowning place of Hungarian kings, the new facility is designed by architect Bela Pinter, and will use the tower as a restaurant. The extension is to be faced in mirrored glass to reflect the site's surrounds.

Howard Johnson has been responsible for conversion of a group of warehouses facing a major canal in Amsterdam into a hotel (this page, center). While both of the last two conversions were motivated by the enforced maintenance of historic buildings and character, other owners are actively seeking conversion of sound structures.

San Francisco's Stanford Court Hotel (photo second from bottom) has been recently stripped of fire escapes and completely refurbished by architects Curtis & Davis. It capitalizes on the popularity of other older hotels in the city. An older conversion, El Convento in San Juan (bottom photo) was an early indicator of the success of the approach. Fortunately, for a diversity of character, for urban cohesion and for the climate of today's economy, recycling has become a tested route to new hotels—and to new architectural commissions.

Habitation Leclerc was once the house of Napoleon's sister. Capitalizing on a spectacular location outside of Port-au-Prince, Haiti and on its historic associations, this resort has been designed to appeal to both Americans and Europeans of affluence—who come just to relax. Here, reuse of an existing structure has provided the real "rooted" atmosphere that other hotel owners have failed to capture from whole fabric. The original house contains the public rooms. Forty-four linked cottages (photo, below) accommodate the guests and have been snaked around existing terraces and vegetation. Louvered doors open the generous rooms (photo, below right) to the normally near-perfect climate. Furnishings throughout the hotel range from the antique to the contemporary.

Much of the older furniture was found in local markets. Bathtubs and sinks are often exposed to the bedrooms. The popularity of this resort—despite its high rates—illustrates the appeal of older buildings and explodes many myths about what guests really want. Despite the extreme care in siting the new cottages, the over-all construction cost were considerably below those for new construction of equal area. The reception desk, in the original house, is open to the outside and arriving guests (photo, top).

HABITATION LECLERC, Port-au-Prince, Haiti. Architect: *Albert Mangones.* Landscape architect: *Ralph Lee.* Interior consultant: *Lawrence Peabody.* Builder: *Allen Milman.*

11

The owner's need to expand retail facilities approximately tenfold, and maintain an inventory of 1,500 categories of items, caused him to seek new quarters. His desire to stay in the same area and continue serving many architectural offices, advertising agencies and The Art Students League, led to a move across the street into a Gothic Revival-style building.

To save the building's features of vaulted ceilings and ornamental plasterwork, and to allow shoppers to browse and to inspect goods, an open plan, utilizing open display cases, was designed. A simple framing system—composed of pipe scaffolding—was installed throughout, but concentrated in the main corridor leading from the store's entrance, from which are hung colorful graphics, lighting fixtures and signs guiding shoppers to the main departments.

Three basic departments (framing, fine arts, technical and commercial) are separated. The type of merchandise dictates its location: easily damaged goods (e.g., papers, boards) were placed behind counters; the framing department was set apart on a carpeted island for quiet; and the commercial art section was centered near the main corridor.

To meet budgetary demands and to have easily maintainable space, durable materials, including ceramic tile flooring and plasterboard walls, were chosen. Pegboard walls in some areas add flexibility in the use of graphics and display capabilities. Acoustical tile was used on flat ceilings to the right and left of entrance for noise control. Most lighting is fluorescent, augmented with incandescent.

LEE'S ART SHOP, New York, New York. Architects: *Macfadyen/De Vido Architects*. Engineers: *Thornton Lev Zetlin Associates* (structural); *Airvel Corporation* (mechanical); *Hartmann & Concessi* (electrical). Interior design: *Macfadyen/De Vido Architects*. Contractor: *Robert Delia, Inc.*

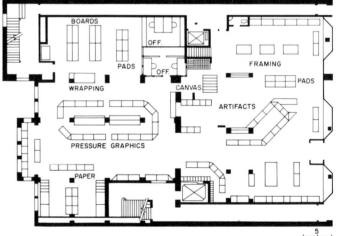

Ed Stoecklein photos

On a long, broken-up front building face (due to building's column), all-glass display windows were extended with angled side panels to attract passers-by from all directions and minimize glare. On both sides of the column, flat windows permit views directly into the store. To unify the exterior with the interiors, three brightly-colored, large pipes were installed above the entrance and display cases. In the rear of the store (far left), vaulting and stained glass windows were not obstructed, and were accented with lights. The framing system is especially prevalent at entrance (below) and in corridor (opposite).

Restoration
and Preservation
of Historic Buildings

The restoration of historic buildings is a special field of architecture, very different from the rehabilitation and remodeling of old structures, although restoration may involve these as well. How much of each process is called for in bringing a historic building back to life depends on two primary considerations: the degree of significance that attaches to the *exact* reproduction of every detail in the building, and the use to which the building will be put in its restored form.

If the building is to be continued in its original use, some modifications will be needed to allow for the amenities of modern life and to permit the installation of up-to-date technological improvements, and these will have to be done without major changes in the original character of the building. At the same time, the building will have to meet code requirements for structure, fire and sanitation.

If the building is to be a museum, what kind of museum it is to be will be an important facet of its restoration. The old Patent Building in Washington, D.C., has become a museum (which in part it always was) for today's use—it is now the Fine Arts/Portrait Gallery—but the building is in itself a museum object. The Gallier house in New Orleans is even more a museum in itself, an artifact, no longer a residence, in fact. Visitor facilities for the Gallier house are provided in an adjacent building which has been remodeled for that purpose, but in the Patent Building, their provision was more a matter of modernization and enlargement. The Renwick Gallery, always a museum (except for its use as a warehouse during the Civil War), is still a museum, with some spaces—the lobby and grand stairway—fully restored, and the galleries handled as an evocation of the period of its origin, rather than as an exact replica.

Full restoration to the original state is a meticulous process, but not without its own brand of excitement. To discover the actual original state of a building often takes real detective work, and often laboratory methods are important in getting at the facts: At Iolani Palace, for example, it took chemical analysis to determine the true answer to duplicating the gold-finished picture rail in the royal chambers, which turned out not to be gold leaf at all. In Louis Sullivan's Chicago Auditorium, faithful adherence to exact reproduction yielded unexpected benefits in uncovering the original paint and samples of Sullivan's unique stencilled ornament.

In only a few cities on this continent have there been efforts to preserve historic sections of the city, but few of these have entailed the extensive restoration undertaken in Montreal's La Place Royale. As an example of cooperation between city agencies and private enterprise it is exceptional, offering an encouraging and useful model to other communities, large and small, for preserving, in more than isolated buildings, the priceless, three-dimensional record of their history.

1

Restoring any building is an exacting process, but restoring a building of historic or architectural significance requires all the art and science at an architect's command. At every step, another person's ideas and another era's ways must govern. There is no room for ego in a good restoration. The satisfaction of rescuing an important building from oblivion and of association with the work of some long-gone master architect offsets the challenge of such a disciplined procedure. But there is far more to restoration than mere duplication of another's work: the right decisions, the careful judgments, demand insight and imagination, and getting at the facts themselves can be as exciting as unraveling a mystery.

To restore a building, however, it must first be saved from whatever ravages threaten it—termites, weather, vandalism, or the ultimate destruction of a wrecking crew—and that takes money. Since there will never be enough money, public or private, to preserve all the worthy buildings, let alone to restore them, those of greatest historical or architectural importance and significance must be the chosen.

The Patent Office Building (right), Washington, D.C., now the National Collection of Fine Arts and the National Portrait Gallery, is a remarkable building, exhibiting the changing tastes of an eventful 27-year period in the development of the United States. Four architects of note contributed to its Greek Revival design, one of the handsomest buildings (and certainly one of the largest in this country) of this architectural style. In its new role of sheltering two art galleries, the old building makes a remarkable come-back, thanks to sensitive and skillful treatment.

Norman McGrath photos

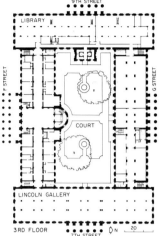

The original building of the old Patent Office was Greek Revival, and this has survived as its exterior character. But when two wings, destroyed by fire, were rebuilt in 1877, the interiors of these sections were done to newer tastes: the third-floor library (3), with its three tiers of reading areas and stacks, is an example of the eclectic design of that day. The burned wings had roofs supported by iron trusses and vaults, instead of the masonry vaults and wood roofs used by Robert Mills in the first two wings which did not burn. The building was designed with great halls (for display of patent models), one of which was the scene of the inaugural ball for Lincoln's second presidential term (2). Its 28 freestanding square marble columns and four pilasters, of unusual and original design, support a series of groined vaults 300 feet long.

THE FINE ARTS-PORTRAIT GALLERY, Washington, D.C. Owner: *The Smithsonian Institution.* Architects: *William P. Eliot, Ithiel Town, Robert Mills, Thomas U. Walter* (original); *Faulkner, Stenhouse, Fryer & Faulkner* (restoration); *Victor Proetz, Bayard Underwood,* consultants. Engineers: *Gongwer & Kraas* (structural); *Wilbending Company, Inc., Egli & Gompf* (mechanical). Lighting consultant: *Stanley R. McCandless.* Landscape architect: *Lester A. Collins.* General contractor: *Grunley-Walsh Construction Co.*

The Renwick Gallery was begun in 1859 as the original Corcoran Gallery of Art. Before it could open it was seized by the Union Army quartermaster corps for use as a Civil War clothing warehouse and did not open as an art gallery until 1871. Later the collection was moved to the present Corcoran Gallery and in 1899 the building became the U.S. Court of Claims.

2

When the Court moved out in 1964, the building stood crumbling. In the same year, John Carl Warnecke's firm had produced a feasibility study of the restoration and rehabilitation of Lafayette Square. Included in the extensive study of the area was the old Court of Claims, which had been retained as a stylistic complement to the Executive Office Building across the street. (Both are excellent adaptations of the French Second Empire style which architect James Renwick used for the first time in the United States in his design for this building.) Warnecke's firm urged that the old Court of Claims be returned to its original function, that of an art gallery.

In 1965 President Johnson approved the transfer of the building to the Smithsonian and restoration began shortly thereafter. Warnecke's firm made the basic interior renovations, replacing the plumbing, wiring, heating and ventilating systems, as well as strengthening the structure in critical areas and removing the various partitions installed by the Court of Claims.

More than a century of weathering had obliterated at least 90 per cent of the original exterior ornament. A joint research team staffed by Warnecke and Universal Restoration Inc. researched various archives to find illustrations of the lost ornamentation, and succeeded in uncovering in the Library of Congress photos taken by Matthew Brady, as well as Renwick's original drawings. Hand carved models were made from blow-ups of the drawings and photos and latex molds were made from these. The new exterior ornamentation is actually a cast composite containing crushed particles of the previously removed stonework, which blends extremely well in color and texture with the older portions of the building.

Hugh Newell Jacobsen & Associates won the commission to further restore the interior in the spirit of Renwick's time. It has been refurbished with period furniture of the last third of the 19th century. Several of the rooms, including the Grand Salon (opposite page) and the Octagon Room (overleaf), are designed as permanent exhibitions. The paintings in the Grand Salon include many which were displayed there almost a century ago when the building served as the original Corcoran Gallery. The works are on loan from the new Corcoran.

The Renwick has no collections of its own. In addition to the two great rooms which are its permanent displays, it will hold design exhibitions of all kinds.

Many years elapsed from the time architect James Renwick finished his design for the original Corcoran Gallery of Art to its completion as a museum, and during this period he had gone out of fashion as an architect. While he was responsible for shaping the noble interior spaces of the gallery, he subsequently had little influence on the interior finishes of the building or the selection of furnishings. Nonetheless, even without the Renwick touch, the 19th-century interiors of the Corcoran represented the epitome of the taste of the time. Architect Hugh Jacobsen's task was not to reproduce these interiors but to evoke them, which he has done with great skill. In the process he came to admire Renwick's ingenious manipulation of scale. "Renwick wanted to make the person smaller, the building grander" says Jacobsen. "Although 8-inch baseboards are customary, some of Renwick's are 14 inches. His chair rails are not all at the usual 36 inches. Some are 30, 48 or even 52 inches." The main foyer and stairs (opposite page, above) have the dark brown wainscoting, light beige walls and ochre trim which was typical of the period. The stair leads directly to the Grand Salon (above). In this room, which is also used for presidential receptions for dignitaries staying at the adjacent Blair House, the paintings are hung on plum colored walls in tiers, just as they were over one hundred years ago. The gigantic urns are from the Philadelphia Centennial Exposition of 1876. Unlike the Grand Salon and the Octagonal Room (overleaf), the remaining galleries will not be restored to their past grandeur as permanent exhibitions in themselves but will be used for changing exhibits (opposite page, bottom left). Such rooms are painted in white or light tones and their moldings and other architectural details are not emphasized by color accents as they are elsewhere. These rooms are high-ceilinged, spacious and filled with daylight.

The Octagonal Room (above) is centered on the main staircase opposite the Grand Salon which can be seen in the photo (above left) taken from the Octagonal Room. The latter space is directly above the entrance foyer and its dome is expressed on the exterior by the central, curved mansard roof. Befitting its importance in the overall spatial hierarchy of the building, including its axial relationship with the Grand Salon, it too has received full and elegant restoration to the gilded age. By deliberate contrast, the stairhall itself, like the foyer below, is of a subdued beige color, its ornament accented only by a change to ochre. The bottom photograph was taken soon after the old Court of Claims moved out and just before renovation.

3

Since 1935, the Historic American Buildings Survey of the National Park Service has measured, photographed and recorded data on historic buildings, and now has accumulated such material on over 15,000 buildings and has placed it in its archives in the Library of Congress.

Among the buildings measured by HABS is Iolani Palace in Honolulu, the last royal residence of the kings of Hawaii. The Palace, used since 1895 as the seat of government, first of the Territory, then of the State, of Hawaii, is in process of restoration to the splendor it had in the last years of the monarchy (1882–1893) when it was new. The original plans of the Palace have not been found, although a notion persists that they are in the cornerstone. Continuing research in the building and excavation of the grounds to determine actual site use, plus the HABS documents, are providing the basis for decisions on the restoration. Paint samples, analyzed for color and chemical content, have yielded unexpected information: for instance, instead of gold leaf having been used on the picture rails as had been believed, orange shellac over tin alloy leaf had produced the effect, and this was easily and (more important) inexpensively restored. Funds for the project are from HUD and the State, and are administered by a nonprofit organization, the Friends of Iolani Palace. The project was begun in 1969 and will take some years to complete.

Iolani Restoration Project

Geoffrey W. Fairfax

Palace life in monarchy will be recreated. First room finished is in Queen's suite.

IOLANI PALACE, Honolulu, Hawaii. Architects: *Thomas J. Baker, Charles J. Wall, Isaac Moore* (original); *Geoffrey W. Fairfax* (restoration). Engineers: *J. Brian Hughes & Assocs., Inc.* (structural); *Howard Hole & Assocs., Inc.* (mechanical); *Bennett & Drane* (electrical); *Walter Lum & Associates* (soil).

4

Adler & Sullivan's unique and **great Auditorium Theater in Chicago** had been badly misused for 25 years before its restoration, and in fact had barely escaped demolition. To bring it back to its original form was more a matter of renovation and repair than of reconstruction, for the building proved, after careful structural inspection and analysis, to be basically sound. One truss was found to have become overstressed because of settling, and this was strengthened. The stage floor was replaced (it had been used as a bowling alley during World War II when the theater was a USO Center) and new fans and heating and cooling coils were installed to work with the original duct system. The remarkable stage equipment—Adler's genius showed here as in the heating and air conditioning system he devised—was in surprisingly good condition, considering its years of disuse and misuse. New stage lighting was required; new ropes for scenery placement, restoration of some of the hydraulic lifts, new dressing rooms and new plumbing were provided. The major costs, however, were for plaster repair, paint and a new electrical system. There were unexpected rewards for faithful adherence to the original plans: When a row of boxes, installed between the orchestra seats and the grand foyer were removed to restore the continuity between theater area and foyer, excellently preserved examples of the original paint and Sullivan's beautiful stencilling were found. The faithful restoration included new chairs in the original design, a duplication of the red carpet Sullivan had designed, even the same kind of long carbon-filament light bulbs that had made the "Golden Arches" scintillate.

The successful restoration of the Auditorium Theater, a demanding and difficult job because of a tight budget, was due to the careful research of the building's original condition, the repair and reconditioning of every possible part of the theater, and the replacement of only those parts (missing plaster ornament, for instance) that could not be repaired. To replace the theater today, with its superb acoustics, its unimpaired sightlines, its array of stage equipment, would cost $16 million, estimates Harry Weese, the restoration architect. But if it had been replaced, there would have been no living record of the genius of Adler, the virtuosity of Sullivan and the techniques of the late 19th century. The Theater's stage—98 feet in clear width, 87 feet in grid height, 62 feet deep—will make possible performances on the grand scale most theaters cannot accommodate.

THE AUDITORIUM THEATER, Chicago, Illinois. Owner: *The Auditorium Theater Council*. Architects: *Adler & Sullivan* (original); *Harry Weese & Associates* (restoration). Engineers: *Severud Associates; The Engineers Collaborative*. Interiors: *Dolores Miller & Associates*. General contractor: *J. W. Snyder Construction Co.*

ch-Blessing

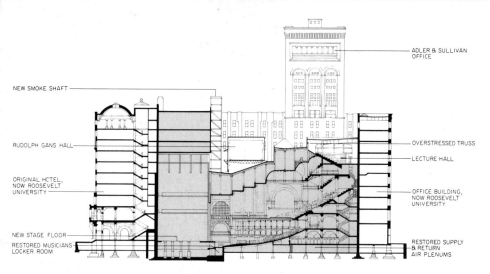

NEW SMOKE SHAFT

RUDOLPH GANS HALL

ORIGINAL HOTEL, NOW ROOSEVELT UNIVERSITY

NEW STAGE FLOOR

RESTORED MUSICIANS LOCKER ROOM

ADLER & SULLIVAN OFFICE

OVERSTRESSED TRUSS

LECTURE HALL

OFFICE BUILDING, NOW ROOSEVELT UNIVERSITY

RESTORED SUPPLY & RETURN AIR PLENUMS

5

The house that an architect designs for himself is always of interest, especially if he is well-known. But the house of a mid-19th century architect is a rare object. The Gallier House in the Vieux Carre of New Orleans was built by James Gallier, Jr., for his family but can be associated with his equally distinguished father, also an architect, since the father lived for 11 years after the house was completed in 1857. Renovated and some parts remodeled for private owners a few years ago, the house has now been restored to its state when new and furnished with objects that closely match those owned by the Galliers. This work was done for the Ella West Freeman Foundation which now administers the house as an historic house museum. The Foundation acquired two adjacent properties to provide facilities necessary to public use (elevator, stairs, coffee shop, ticket desk) which would otherwise have had to be inserted in the Gallier House. This adjacent building also contains displays of objects belonging to the two architects and pertaining to their profession.

Restoration of the Gallier House was greatly facilitated by access to the original working drawings, now deposited at Tulane University, to old photographs and to an annotated plan describing the original heating and plumbing equipment. Not all restoration architects are so fortunate, and many find the first thing required is to make measured drawings of the building, a delaying and often expensive process.

Frank Lotz Miller

2

3

The Gallier House, as elegant and dignified now as it was 100 years ago, was restored without visitor facilities—since these could be located in the adjacent building, renovated to provide exhibition space and a controlled entrance to the Gallier House. The façade of the exhibition building was restored (5), but the interior has been remodeled and the warehouse of which it had long been a part was demolished, opening up an alley to a rare commodity in the French Quarter: parking space (3). On the other side of the alley is the twin of the exhibition building, available for expansion when needed.

JAMES GALLIER, JR., HOUSE, New Orleans, Louisiana. Owner: *The Ella West Freeman Foundation.* Architects: *James Gallier, Jr.* (original); *Richard Koch and Samuel Wilson, Jr.* (restoration). Engineers: *A. W. Thompson & Associates* (structural); *Warren G. Moses* (mechanical / electrical). Landscape architect: *Christopher C. Friedrichs; Richard Koch & Samuel Wilson, Jr.* General contractor: *Haase Construction Company.*

5

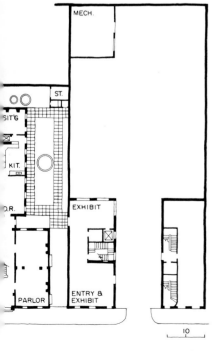

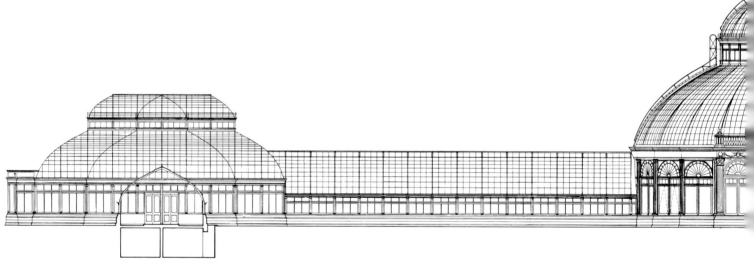

The Conservatory of the New York Botanical Garden in the Bronx is a remarkable building begun in 1899. It was inspired by the Great Palm House at the Royal Botanic Gardens at Kew, England built between 1845 and 1847 by Decimus Burton in the Italian Renaissance style. Other precedents for its design were Sir Joseph Paxton's Crystal Palace built for the 1851 Great Exhibition in London. A building designed for the New York Exhibition of 1853 with a dome at its crossing might also have been a precedent. The Bronx Conservatory is believed to have been designed by William R. Cobb, architect for Lord & Burnham, then and now prominent manufacturers of greenhouses.

The photographs on this and the opposite page show the building as it appeared shortly after 1902. Although severely mutilated by insensitive restoration in 1938 and 1953 (see photographs on the next pages), it still possesses its great double dome and cupola, its cruciform corner pavilions and handsome apses.

The structure is now being extensively restored as part of an overall scheme for the physical improvement of the entire garden. The work is being done under the direction of architect Edward Larrabee Barnes and his associate, Alistair Bevington; and landscape architect Dan Kiley and his partner Peter Ker Walker who are restudying the garden.

The drawing above shows the proposed restoration of the ornamentation on the central domed pavilion. The wings and cruciform pavilions will remain unadorned (they lost their original filigree in the 1938 reconstruction and repair performed by the Department of Parks, and the cost of replacement is prohibitive). Two wooden vestibules which face the garden will be restored to their 1902 appearance.

According to Siglinde Stern, project architect for the Conservatory reconstruction, the work of restoration has been exceedingly difficult because the original Lord & Burnham drawings cannot be found. They were believed

The Conservatory, begun in 1899, was once richly ornamented, as the photos above and below, taken in 1902, indicate. As will be seen in the photographs on the next two pages, virtually all of this ornamentation has been destroyed partly by aging, but chiefly by blundering attempts to improve the building in 1938 and 1953. Because of limited funds, the current restoration will include only repairs to the building's structural and mechanical system, replacement of broken glass and the reconstruction of the ornamentation of the central domed pavilion as shown in the drawing below. Two small vestibules facing the Conservatory terrace will also be reconstructed. The interior partitions will be restored to their original beauty.

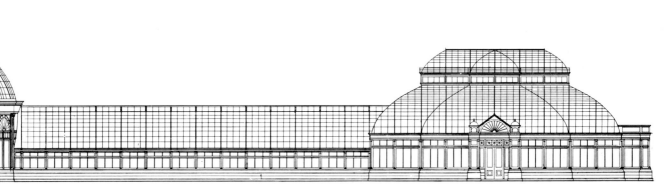

to have been lost in a Parks Department cleanup in 1933. She has resorted to measured drawings which were made in 1938 in preparation for that remodeling and has used old photographs like the ones on these pages for detail.

First priority has been given to arresting the rapidly progressing deterioration of the building. Defective and corroded members of the steel superstructure will be replaced. The glass skin and all its parts, such as the rafter bars and glazing bars, will be replaced or repaired as required. The defective roof and sidewall ventilators will be replaced or repaired. The existing steam heating system will

be replaced, the entire building rewired and new water supply piping and new floor drains installed.

The photographs above show the extent to which the building has been damaged by inept remodeling as well as decay and neglect. The south entrance to the central domed pavilion (directly above) which was perpetrated by the Parks Department in 1953 will be removed, as will the brick wall and waterfall (also the work of the fifties) at what was once the north entrance (top right). The original cast iron façades and interior vestibules will be reconstructed at these locations. The wood vestibules were altered in 1938 (opposite page, top) and the two

which face the Conservatory terrace will be restored to their original rather exotic appearance. (They never went very well with the Italian Renaissance façades of the central pavilion as can be seen in the photo overleaf, but their restoration will summon forth the genial spirit of eclecticism which graced so many turn-of-the-century buildings designed for pleasure.)

Badly damaged or missing are the wood and glass partitions which separate the various elements of the Conservatory. These will also be reconstructed. The arched transoms in the central domed pavilion which were crudely simplified in the 1938 restoration (top left) will

be rebuilt with the delicate ornamentation of the original design.

As shocking as the mutilating additions is the present planting scheme for the Conservatory courtyard (above) and the terrace at the rear. These elements are being restudied as part of the overall master plan for the horticultural design and development of the grounds. The Conservatory courtyard will become a site primarily devoted to the interests of city gardeners who garden in pots, tubs, boxes and other containers. Included will be a wide variety of trees, shrubs and flowering plants, topiary and other trained specimens, as well as vegetable gardens to educate, stimulate

The central domed pavilion was left relatively intact (opposite page, top left) during the 1938 restoration, except for the arched transoms which were crudely simplified, but the vestibules were remodeled badly (right). This restoration, however, saved the building, for important structural and mechanical repairs were made at the time. The 1958 remodeling (opposite page, top right and below) was a total disaster. The terrace entrance to the conservatory was walled up and the wall became a back drop for an ill-conceived fountain. A "modernistic" entrance vestibule was applied to the courtyard side and clumps of bushes were planted to conceal the building's curves.

and encourage everyone interested in city garden methods and techniques.

The restoration also reflects the fact that the New York Botanical Garden is not exclusively an institution for botanical research, but, as Garden president Dr. Howard S. Irvin points out "is a great public amenity and a recreational resource for New Yorkers and visitors from all over the world." Until now the Conservatory building has been a greenhouse for the plants which Dr. Irwin calls "the tough survivors"—those which were able to stand the overheating in its not-too-sensitive environment. The new improvements in climate control will permit a far greater variety of plants

and greater flexibility in topical and seasonal exhibits. In its efforts to reach out to the people of the Bronx community whose brick and concrete neighborhoods offer little by way of trees and grass and where free amenities are limited, the Botanical Garden sees the Conservatory as a stage for special community-oriented events. At the same time, the restoration will provide sufficient flexibility to serve the Garden's public audience which is extremely varied in its interests and knowledge.

While the restoration of the Conservatory has first priority, a new exhibition structure called the Plants and Man Building will eventually be constructed (page 160). Architect

Barnes explains that as the Conservatory is oriented to horticulture, the Plants and Man Building will be directed to botany, ecology and other biological relationships between plants and man. According to the program developed by the Garden, it will include "special examples of plant relationships such as mimicry, plants that grow on other plants, parasitism, insectivorous plants, plant adaptations, and interrelationships between certain plants and animals including, of course, mankind."

As described by Barnes, the Plants and Man Building will be a totally new kind of glass structure. It is composed of hexagonal modules, roughly 45 feet across, that may be

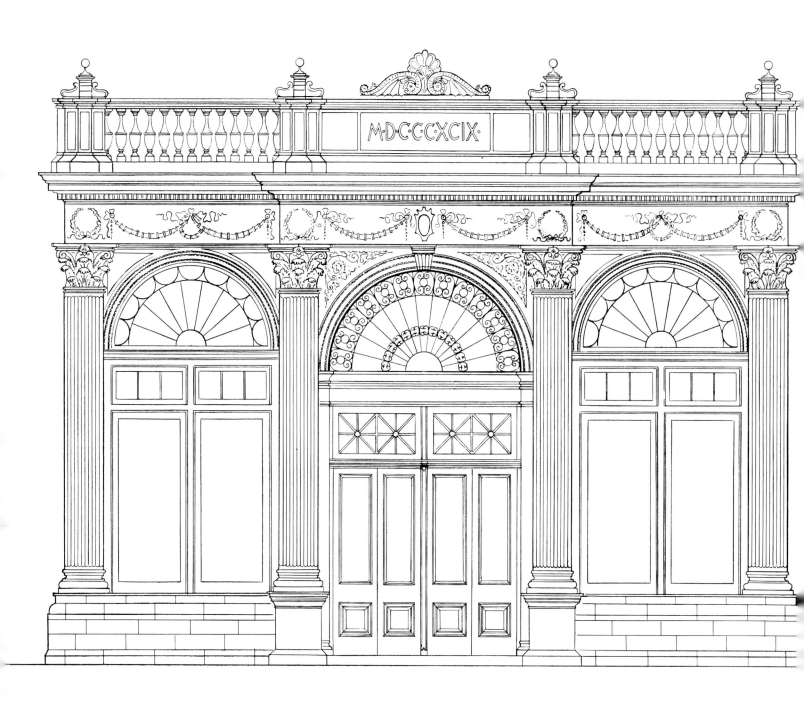

grouped together vertically or horizontally to create a plant system environment of any desired size. The walls of these chambers may expand vertically to accommodate the growth of trees. Each plant system environment would have its own indigenous climate.

The building in plan forms a handsome forecourt which leads to the building entrance and to the garden beyond. This undulating glass structure will not be a closed prismatic form. Infinitely flexible, it will interlock the plants within it with the surrounding landscape. As Barnes points out, the clustering of hexagonal modules has many parallels in nature: the honeycomb, the quartz crystal, the microscopic plant structure itself. The hexagon, unlike the octagon and more elaborate geometric shapes, is a nesting form that can be combined simply and repetitively for growth in six directions. Like a beehive, the Plants and Man Building in the years ahead can add new modules as programs change and develop. High and low modules can nest side by side in endless variety.

The supporting structure will be a system of slender pipe columns, tubular beams and diagonal tension rods. The hexagonal roof of each module will slope to a central gutter and internal downspout.

Both the restored Conservatory and the projected Plants and Man Building are the key display areas in a land use plan which will greatly improve the Garden's usefulness as a public educational and recreational resource. In the summertime the Garden serves as one big back yard for people within walking distance in the Bronx. Picnic tables are provided. According to Dr. Irwin, the Garden has a very high standard of maintenance and this in turn encourages its users not to litter or vandalize. In recent years there has been little conflict between the need to protect the Garden and its buildings and plantings and the need to make it free to all as a green oasis in the city and the reasons for that happy truth might well be care-

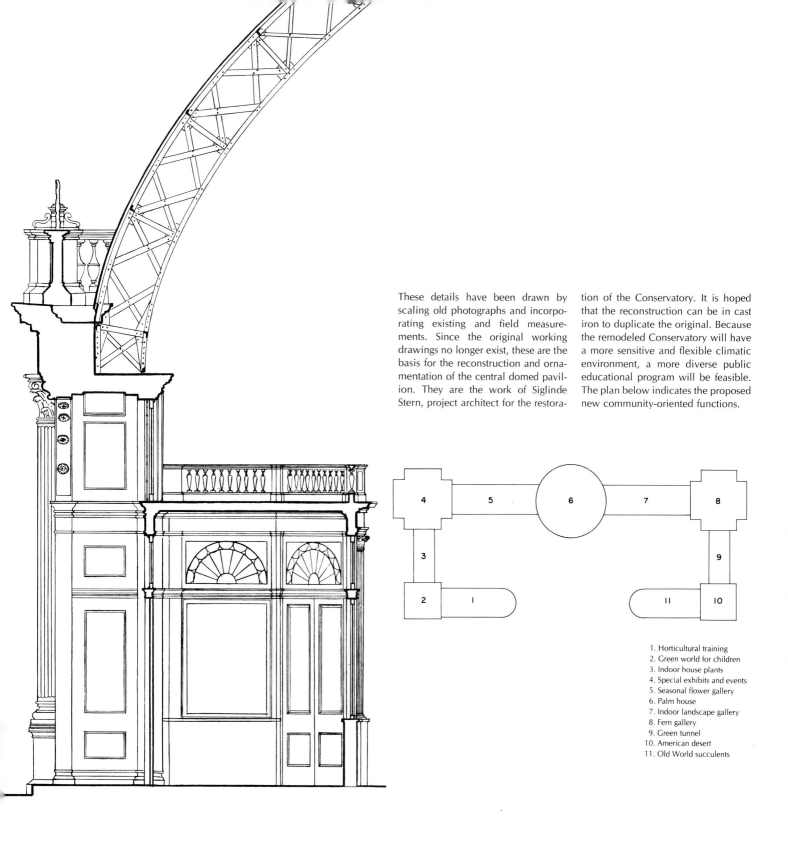

These details have been drawn by scaling old photographs and incorporating existing and field measurements. Since the original working drawings no longer exist, these are the basis for the reconstruction and ornamentation of the central domed pavilion. They are the work of Siglinde Stern, project architect for the restoration of the Conservatory. It is hoped that the reconstruction can be in cast iron to duplicate the original. Because the remodeled Conservatory will have a more sensitive and flexible climatic environment, a more diverse public educational program will be feasible. The plan below indicates the proposed new community-oriented functions.

1. Horticultural training
2. Green world for children
3. Indoor house plants
4. Special exhibits and events
5. Seasonal flower gallery
6. Palm house
7. Indoor landscape gallery
8. Fern gallery
9. Green tunnel
10. American desert
11. Old World succulents

fully studied by other park planners.

The master land use plan for the 250-acre Garden, prepared by architect Barnes with landscape architect Kiley, takes measures to preserve those undeveloped areas best suited as a nature preserve, while making the Conservatory and the projected Plants and Man Building and their surrounding courts and terraces more accessible to the public.

As the present and future land use plans (page 160) indicate, the boundaries of the Garden are redefined. Fencing, pedestrian gateways and major entrances are better related to the most frequently visited areas. A new main entrance and bus and auto drop-off has been designed (see model photograph page 160) which, according to Barnes, has been inspired by the work of Frederick Law Olmsted. As occurs in a number of locations in Central Park, pedestrians will enter a grotto-like tunnel which burrows through a mound and opens into a broad and verdant landscape. The tunnel will heighten the experience of contrast between the world of the Garden and the world of the Bronx. Opening off the tunnel will be sky-lit grotto shaped spaces which will contain a plant and book store, an orientation center, toilets and a guard office.

Within the Garden all unnecessary roads will be eliminated and private cars will be restricted to the peripheral road which gives access to the Conservatory and the Plants and Man Building. This will enhance the attractiveness of the Garden immeasurably, attract bicyclists, encourage people to walk and reduce air pollution. To enable people to visit the more remote parts of the Garden, Barnes and Kiley propose the use of small electric buses which will follow a peripheral route that will circumscribe the outlying natural areas of the Garden and interconnect them with the Conservatory and the Plants and Man Building. To complete this admirable circulation plan, an aerial tramway has been proposed to link the Garden with the Bronx Zoo.

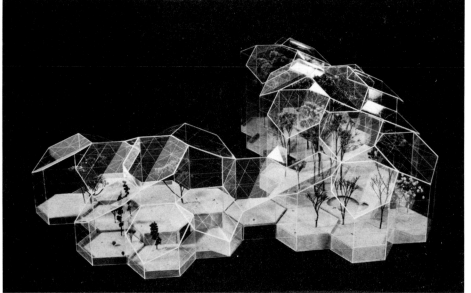

Alistair Bevington

The proposed Plants and Man Building (above and right) will be constructed of hexagonal glass modules. As the new master plan (below right) indicates, circulation by auto and electric mini-bus will be limited to the park perimeter. The interior roadways shown in the existing plan (below left) will be for pedestrian use only. The model photograph (bottom right) is of the proposed new main entrance.

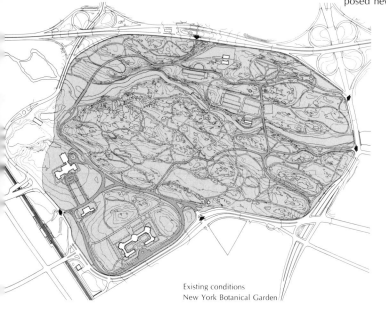

Existing conditions
New York Botanical Garden

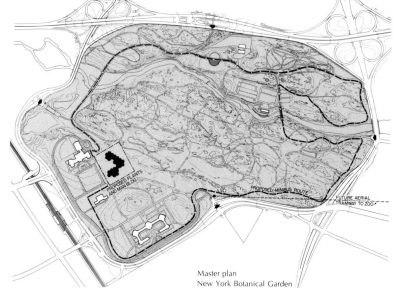

Master plan
New York Botanical Garden

NEW YORK BOTANICAL GARDEN RESTORATION, Bronx, N.Y. Master plan architect: *Edward Larrabee Barnes—associate-in-charge: Alistair Bevington, project architect: David Arnold.* Landscape architect: *Dan Kiley & Partners—partner-in-charge: Peter Ker Walker.* Conservatory restoration architect: *Edward Larrabee Barnes—project architect: Siglinde Stern.* Consultants: *Weidinger Associates* (structural); *Arthur A. Edwards* (mechanical and electrical); *Billie S. Fritz* (industrial archeologist). Plants and Man Building architect: *Edward Larrabee Barnes—associate-in-charge: Alistair Bevington, project architect: David Arnold.* Consultants: *Weidlinger Associates* (structural); *Lehr Associates* (mechanical and electrical).

John V. Y. Lee

160

7

Helena, capital of the state of Montana, is a city of surprises: its main street is called Last Chance Gulch, a name which suggests the wildest and wooliest of western towns; but the street is lined with handsome stone business structures of late Victorian vintage. Its residential district has some of the West's most splendid nineteenth-century mansions, for here the mining barons built their homes, and having much to spend, spared nothing on their residences. But deterioration and change have set in, especially in the business section. A survey of some 90 buildings in the city has been made by architects Jacobson & Shope, and a few of the buildings have been rehabilitated, by the same architects, including the Diamond Block (middle right) and the Old Blue Stone House (two photos, middle left and center).

RESTORATION OF DIAMOND BLOCK and OLD BLUE STONE HOUSE, Helena, Montana. Architects: *Jacobson & Shope*

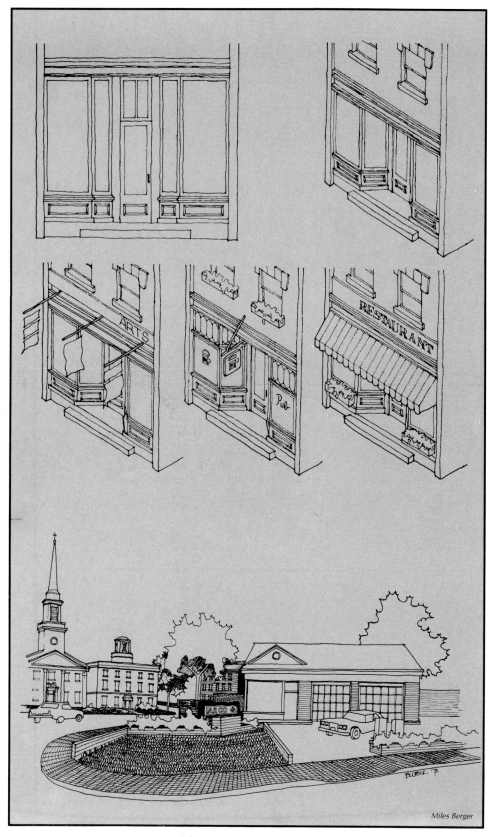

Miles Berger

8

Vision, Inc., a young design firm, is a nonprofit public foundation based in Cambridge, Massachusetts, whose conservation energies are directed into three different realms: advocating community sentiments to planning authorities, counseling corporate clients on the impact their buildings have on towns, and actually designing town preservation schemes.

Vision, Inc., believes and acts on the idea that townscape conservation is an asset to planning; the designs shown here all reflect the conviction that existing towns are basically all right, but superficially marred by garish additions (like big neon signs) or unfortunate subtractions (like buildings torn down to make a parking lot).

Vision feels it has ready solutions. The directions which accompany the proposed storefront details, at left, read: "1. The original design, materials and details should be used wherever possible. 2. A façade should not be made to look older than it actually is; colonial details on a Victorian façade only look artificial and do justice to neither style. 3. The introduction of modern elements to the façade must be done with extreme care so as not to violate the original intent of the building." Similarly, Vision's project for a gas station renovation in Portsmouth, New Hampshire, seeks to tame the building's commercial image by removing the large signs, hiding the pumps behind brick retaining walls, and planting daffodils and chrysanthemums—in some cases the best solution in the world—if the plants are cared for.

All this makes sense, and, at best, the results can be very handsome. It is true that Vision's efforts can be repressive, for, as every good lawyer knows, it is hard to devise a set of clear and simple rules that accommodate the unruliness of human desire, good or bad. But what Vision has done is to highlight the values of existing townscapes, particularly in small towns, which have a rich stock not only for good buildings, but good *places*.

TOWNSCAPE DESIGNS, Portsmouth, New Hampshire, Bellows Falls, Vermont, Exeter, New Hampshire, Middlebury, Vermont. Project consultants: *Vision, Inc.*

Robert Luchetti

Vision's vision for a street corner in Bellows Falls, Vermont, involves the removal of an existing building and replacing it with a small sunken plaza; the building then facing the plaza would sprout an old-fashioned two-story porch, from which its occupants could view the passing pedestrian scene.

The Town Hall of Exeter, New Hampshire, now faces an open parking area; Vision would remove the parking and substitute a park. Note how, in the rendering, power lines have been removed, and how the cacaphonous details of the storefronts have been replaced by visual consistency.

(Above) Thomas Blurock (below) Michael Chan

Middlebury, Vermont, has a familiar snaggle-tooth problem along one of its streets; Vision's designers attempt to fill the gap by planting a row of large trees which (in summer, at least) would continue the line of the building façades along the street.

9

What may prove unique in the restoration of North American historic sites is the rehabilitation of a large section of the lower town of Quebec, called la Place Royale. There work is proceeding steadily towards the reclamation of seventy-seven buildings dating from the 17th and 18th centuries. Six are now open to the public. When completed within a few years, the restoration will recreate the Grand Epoch of old New France.

From an architectural standpoint it is extraordinary to find so many restorable old buildings within a restricted space of approximately 300,000 square feet. This is the more remarkable when it is considered that this section lying along the waterfront on the St. Lawrence River has been subject to continual use and misuse for nearly three centuries.

Despite the area's architectural and historic interest, la Place Royale will not become just another museum. Tenants temporarily displaced will return and occupy living quarters above the first floors of most of the buildings. While there will be antique shops, boutiques, restaurants and craft demonstrations for visitors, emphasis will be on present day living for the actual residents. Thus, in recreating an ancient aspect of Quebec, the planners seek to insure living continuity for the present and the future. It is very probable that the old streets will be filled with youngsters and the day's wash hung from back windows, as in the rest of the lower town (Sous le Cap) under the cliff.

Two things have occurred which make effective restoration possible. All of the extant buildings in the area are stone ones with sound foundations and thick walls. They were built to last by stone masons working in a tradition demanding longevity of structure.

Mr. Goulding is senior vice president of Arthur Schmidt & Associates in New York, and a writer on architectural and historical subjects. He is the author of "The Irish Brigade," "The Providence Arcade," and "New France Preserved." La Place Royale is clearly a great love.

They have withstood bombardments and recurring fires and are still intact as can be seen in the before and after photos of Maison Leduc (figs. 3, 4). Even so, they might long since have fallen victim of demolition crews had not the decline of commercial activity in la Place Royale early in the 19th century discouraged replacement by more modern structures. As matters stand practically no reproduction of buildings will be required, as has been necessary in so many other restoration projects.

The restoration is being financed jointly by the Province of Quebec through the Ministry of Cultural Affairs and the Canadian Government. It has been long in gestation and involves the leading architects of the province as well as other professional, business and intellectual leaders.

Together these have worked out a concept which is now being carried out faithfully. Of this concept the project preamble states:

"Conceived by the coordination bureau of la Place Royale in the Ministry of Cultural Affairs, the general plan, far from being the product of an unbridled imagination, is the result of serious analysis and diligent research, carried on by a multi-professional team.

"La Place Royale being above all an architectural ensemble, the largest number of homes must be preserved. It is important to recreate an atmosphere, to revive the old buildings in a harmonious arrangement and to avoid giving them the uniform appearance of a settled period. This would be artificial and entirely debatable. A lack of documentation and an orderly plan preclude the choice of an architectural remounting beyond the fire of 1682. By setting this date limit, the aim is to constitute all the aspects of traditional Quebec architecture which, for two and one half centuries, has been in the French tradition.

"From 1680 to 1810 a way of building had developed. Unity of style and materials were accepted facts. The character of la Place

Royale was determined by the style of the church and by an architectural rhythm; the unity of the ensemble is indicated by the dimensions of the open spaces. Furthermore, the proportion of solid and open spaces characteristic of a period and a way of building will be regained."

The exteriors of the houses will very exactly conform to the ancient state. The interiors, however, will be treated in a fashion to respond to contemporary needs.

Realism dictated the choice of epoch. There was a desire to push the restoration on further back in history. After all, Quebec is the oldest North American city in continuous occupation north of St. Augustine, Florida. It was established by Samuel de Champlain in 1608, eight years before the founding of New Amsterdam and twelve years before the landing of the Pilgrims at Plymouth Rock. The fire of 1682 was the determinant. It had destroyed the older buildings. Thereafter, these had been replaced by the still standing stone buildings. The venerable church of Notre Dame des Victoires, for example, had been built above the site of Champlain's house and fort.

The other time limit was determined by another catastrophe. In 1759 Wolfe beseiged Quebec. The fleet under Admiral Saunders and the artillery from the heights of Levis across the St. Lawrence had fired more than 30,000 solid shot and 10,000 fire bombs into the upper and lower towns. These had caused a disastrous fire which gutted virtually all buildings. In the rehabilitation which followed, work was continued in the French tradition, but by 1810 this tradition had died out in la Place Royale. Hence the emphasis on the 17th and 18th centuries.

La Place Royale is replete with history. It is the core of that part of the lower town which is still the principal gateway to Quebec for all who come by water (figs. 1, 2). A constant procession of immigrants of both high and low degree have traversed its streets. It has survived onslaughts by the fleets of

Kirk, Phipps and Saunders. Its square witnessed the blessing of le regiment de Carignan Salieres in 1664 when that regiment, the first uniformed force in North America, arrived to rescue New France from the Iroquois menace. Within its borders anxious prospective grooms met the King's girls sent over by Louis XIV to become their wives. Governors and their staffs, bishops and their lesser clergy, visiting foreign diplomats and Indian chiefs, arriving intendants and departing officials, all knew la Place Royale. Each day farmers arrived by river to bring fresh fruits and vegetables, fish and meat for the housewives of Quebec. Ultimately English troops marched through the streets to garrison the heights and, in the early days of the American Revolution, General Montgomery fell nearby under withering musketry when he and Arnold sought to assault the town.

In all the years from 1682 to 1759 la Place Royale was the principal commercial center of Quebec. Government and church had moved up the winding Cote de la Montagne to establish residence in the upper town but prosperous merchants had their headquarters

on the square. These had their stores on the first floors of the stout stone buildings, and lived with their families above and in the formal gardens to the rear.

It was when the merchants began to desert the area in the early 19th century that la Place Royale began to take on that aspect of decay so well known to tourists in this century. While it always ·retained its charm and picturesque quality, neglect caused decay and dilapidation. Now that is being corrected.

As the merchants moved away, their former residences began to serve other purposes. Attracted by low rentals the upper floors swiftly filled with low-income families. Apartments were divided and sub-divided by landlords to serve more and more people. Retail stores moved into the area to serve them. Walls were pierced to install show windows. The waterfront was still active. Ship's chandlers and other outfitters took over many of the lower floors. The back rooms of many buildings were used as store rooms. Restaurants and saloons to serve seamen ashore sprang up.

As time went on, façades were variously painted and coated with stucco and cement and the old stone walls were hidden from view. Some windows were blocked up and others made their appearance. Casement windows gave way to double hung, single paned ones. Upper stories with flat roofs were added to some structures. In many instances walls were broken through to combine two or three buildings. When fire in 1965 gutted Hotel Louis XIV at the north end of la Place Royale it was discovered that the hotel comprised two adjoining buildings (figs 5,6).

Abuse and neglect by successive landlords and tenants during the 19th century completed dilapidation. The historic and architectural merit of la Place Royale, nonetheless, never was completely forgotten. As early as 1929 Notre Dame des Victoires was declared a national monu-

ment and a movement got underway to extend rehabilitation of the area. In 1960 a nationally known architect, M. Pierre Robitaille, was retained by the Quebec Commission of Historic Monuments to study the old façades. His encouraging recommendations were adopted by the commission and the Municipal Council of Quebec. The Province, encouraged by the federal government at Ottawa, undertook the work, placing supervision in the Ministry of Cultural Affairs, where it reposes. Successive ministers directing the project have been M. Pierre Laporte, Francois Cloutier and the present minister, Madame Claire Kirkland-Casgrain. The Ministry's Department of Architecture is in charge of operations with Maurice Laperriere as chief and Jacques le Barbanchon assistant chief. Staff architects are Jean-Louis Boucher, Albert Dehin and Guy Chenevert. Architectural students in all the provincial universities are engaged in detailed drawings.

Consulting architects are Dorval and Fortin, Laroche, Ritchot and Dery, Lavigne and Marquis, Dupre and Voyer, and Pierre Cantin, all of Quebec City, and Jacques Ayotte of Montreal. Scharry and Ouimet of Quebec and Montreal are mechanical and electrical engineers and Vandry, Jobin and Associates of Quebec are construction engineers.

Architects and engineers are fulfilling the long wished for restoration of old Quebec and archaeologists, historians, archivists, librarians, art leaders and leaders of the business community are also involved.

Plans for la Place Royale include an area 500 feet wide and 600 feet long. It is bounded on the north by la Cote de la Montagne, which winds up the cliff to the upper town. La rue Champlain on which Maison Chevalier sits is its southern boundary. To the east it faces the waterfront and to the west it backs up against the foot of the cliff. The old streets and lanes, which remain unchanged from early days, are presently covered

11

with asphalt, but will be paved with stone blocks when restoration is complete. All electrical, gas and communication lines will be laid underground and the streets will be lighted by old types of lamps. It is possible that the area of work may be extended.

Intensive research and analysis preceded any demolition. This was conducted in the archives of Quebec, Montreal and Ottawa, in museums and libraries, and at the ancient Seminaire de Quebec. Old records were examined in the Paris Archives Nationales, and at the Library of Congress in Washington, and in a period of a few years a vast accumulation of books, military and civil records, paintings, portraits, pen and ink sketches, architectural drawings, family histories, private journals, correspondence and business records came into being.

So exhaustive was the search that the Ministry of Cultural Affairs was able to reconstruct the history of original builders and occupiers of the old houses together with those of their successors. In many cases architectural plans were found which permitted utmost accuracy in restoration work.

The result of this research was an overabundance of material confronting architects and others working on the project. Painstaking sifting and selection solved these problems only to have the architects confronted with another problem; the condition of extant buildings. It became necessary to strip each to the bare walls.

Prior to demolition the Province found temporary living quarters for the tenants and then the archaeologists began a search from attics to cellars. A large accumulation of artifacts was uncovered in this search. They have been catalogued and most of them are now on display. They include more than one dozen large copper kettles, many wine bottles with the wine still in them, much porcelain, ceramics and glassware from various periods, 18th-century clothing, many buttons, a number of coins including one dated 1586, cannon and musket balls and one fire bomb. Some cannon balls were found embedded in façades facing the waterfront, and these have been left in place.

Demolition crews work from the rooftops downwards. Added upper stories are entirely removed and care is taken to retain or rebuild the slope of roofs as revealed by the original gables. All encrustations on exterior and interior façades are stripped away. This includes inner partitions installed by successive generations. Wherever possible all salvagable material is retained for use in construction. Planking laid down over the original wide floor beams is removed and in many instances these old planks are found to be sound and hence serviceable. The curves of some very charming staircases have been rescued. In nearly every original room fireplaces have been discovered and reopened.

All demolition is under the supervision of architects as is the necessary repair work on foundations and walls. Architects also supervise inspections to insure prevention of future fires and possible building collapse. All stonework is cleaned, polished and

pointed up and all joining rigidly secured.

Maison Chevalier (fig. 11) has served as a model for successful reconstruction elsewhere. This structure proved to be three adjoining stone buildings. As it stands with three sides facing the waterfront at the extreme end of the la Place Royale Restoration, Maison Chevalier reveals noble proportions in all its aspects. The interior walls are of white plaster with windows framed in the 18th-century style. The wide floor boards glisten with beeswax, hand applied. The ceilings show adz and old saw marks on the exposed beams. In such a setting the 17th- and 18th-century Canadian pine armoires stand in sharp contrast to the white walls. In room after room old tables, chairs, beds and other furniture and furnishings exhibit the craftsmanship of ancient cabinet makers who simplified early French models using native goods to create a distinctly Canadian style (figs. 7,8,9,10). Elsewhere framed documents, portraits of early settlers, pen and ink sketches by military artists, maps, sculpture, appliances and tools convincingly portray how life was lived in old Quebec.

Fascinating to watch is the manner in which modern workmen, more used to power tools than hand tools, have been trained to employ old methods of construction. This is especially noteworthy even in roof timbers which are to be hidden. Although invisible the joining utilizes techniques consistent with earlier centuries (figs. 12, 13).

The work of restoration has proceeded to a point where architects visiting Quebec this year may observe progress in all phases from demolition to completed restoration (figs. 14, 15, 16).

Completion of la Place Royale is some years away. It will include a reproduction of the old ramparts which once faced the harbor. Instead of cannon, however, there will be trees and benches for the benefit of residents and visitors. While the needs of residents will

be given first consideration, the Ministry of Cultural Affairs is well aware of the attraction the section will hold for tourists. As one member remarked, ''Visitors do not come to Quebec to see our skyscrapers.'' This realistic attitude reflects restorations proceeding elsewhere in Quebec. As a result it is most probable that la Place Royale will become, as its promoters desire, one of the outstanding historical attractions of North America.

Additions Designed for Neighborhood Preservation

When an old building can continue in use only if more space can be added to it, the question that invariably presents itself is: should the addition exactly duplicate in architectural style the original building? Or should it be designed in a modification of that style—or should it forget the past and express itself, a contemporary building designed and built to contemporary standards? A case can be made for each approach. But in the hands of a skillful and talented architect, a fourth alternative is possible. Each of the buildings in this chapter illustrates this last approach—a sensitive and understanding response to the *essence* of the older building's architectural concept. The additions make no bones about being new and contemporary, but they just as clearly state their relation to (and sometimes their dependency on) the existing building by subtly echoing the earlier design, using the same finish material, or aligning openings and eaves, or adopting or adapting the old details in new ways.

Additions sometimes take the form of whole new buildings, or are of such size and scope that they have the effect of new entities in a neighborhood. What is added to a neighborhood can make or break its character, especially if the area contains an architecturally significant building. One of modern architecture's significant landmarks, the Philadelphia Savings Fund Society "skyscraper" of 1930, could have been gravely affected by a new building immediately next to it if the new building had been indifferent to the architectural statement of PSFS. Fortunately, PSFS was treated with great respect, to the benefit of the whole block.

Preserving the context of a neighborhood—its scale, its character, its uses—is an enhancement to the newcomer building as well as to the existing area, as in the case of the New York Bar Center, where a row of rehabilitated houses form the street face of the Center, with the new buildings, carefully designed to fit the existing scale, located behind.

Adding onto a building or inserting a new building into an old neighborhood demands sensitivity on the part of both client and architect, and a skill that is peculiarly the architect's to contribute. The quality of the cityscape is either made or unmade by the sense it evokes of a concern for the impact of the built environment on the human beings who pass through it and use it.

1

The new Cleveland Trust Company Tower preserves an important city landmark while at the same time it reinforces and invigorates its urban setting. The decision to preserve the original banking building erected in 1907 meant the permanent dedication to the city of the air space above this structure. Only the first stage of the tower has been built so far. The future wing can be seen in the plans (opposite page, bottom). The tower's 1,314 precast concrete panels of grey Vermont granite aggregate form a non-absorptive surface which discourages the accumulation of soot and dirt. As the details (below) indicate, the inside corners have been rounded so as to eliminate dirt-catching crevices. This self-cleaning design includes channels for rainwater chased into the outside edges of the panels. By means of this device, rainwater never drains across more than one panel, thus eliminating staining. The building will weather more evenly, from top to bottom.

THE CLEVELAND TRUST COMPANY HEADQUARTERS, Cleveland, Ohio. Architects: *Marcel Breuer and Hamilton Smith; associated architects for local supervision: Flynn, Dalton, Van Dijk & Partners.* Engineers: *Weidlinger Associates* (structural); *Barber & Hoffman* (soil), *H. W. H. Associates* (mechanical/electrical). Consultants: *Lewis S. Goodfriend and Associates* (acoustical); *David Mintz Lighting Associates* (lighting); *Frazier, Orr, Fairbank & Quam Inc.* (interior design); *Sandgren and Murtha, Inc.* (graphics); *Raymond C. Daly* (general construction); *Norwell Burgess* (bank operations). General contractor: *Turner Construction Company.*

Erol Akyavas photos

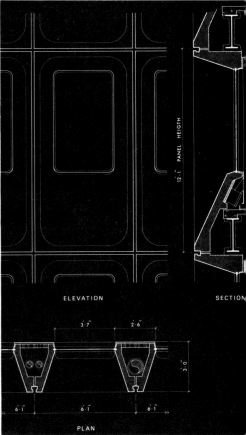

1 Entrance lobby
2 Connection to existing corner bank
3 Banking lobby
4 Clerical
5 Storage
6 Truck dock
7 Receiving

8 Existing corner bank
9 Second-phase construction
10 Meeting room foyer
11 Meeting room
12 Infirmary
13 Balcony connection
14 Office space

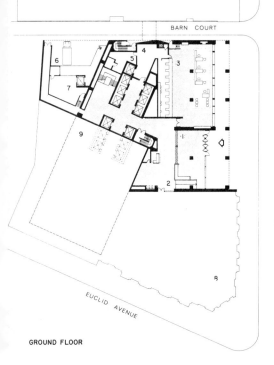

GROUND FLOOR

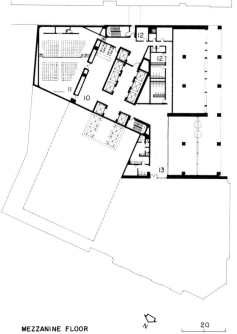

MEZZANINE FLOOR

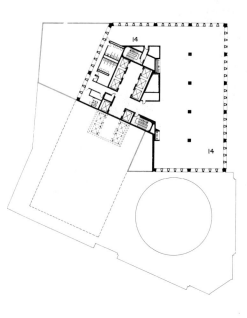

TYPICAL FLOOR

2

The first major building in Philadelphia's Market Street East Transportation Mall Center—a 20-story glass-walled office building—is an excellent example of design which gives equal attention to the old neighbors (one an important architectural milestone) of the new building and to the integrity of the new building itself, a clearly contemporary design solution.

On one side of 1234 Market Street East, the new building, is a 1930 architectural landmark, the Philadelphia Savings Fund Society Building of George Howe and William Lescaze, significant for its time not only as skyscraper design but also as an expression of the best in architecture of that period. On the other side is the much earlier John Wanamaker department store, a handsome building of classic derivation.

Between these two strongly individual and richly atmospheric buildings, 1234 Market East makes a quiet but confident architectural statement of its own time. The glass façade, clear at the base where the public spaces are located and dark for all the floors above, is so restrained and simple that it allows both older buildings to stand in undiminished dignity, respectfully observing the proportions and the lines of its neighbors without in any way diminishing itself.

In other ways, not visible from the street, 1234 Market East fits into its neighborhood, not only as it is, but as it is coming to be. The building, because of its location in Philadelphia's big Transportation Mall Center project (RECORD, April 1974, pages 146-149), acts as a link in the three-level pedestrian walkway system which leads to a variety of transportation means, and along a skylighted shopping mall. It also connects with the PSFS Building (its original design had anticipated a below-grade concourse) and the Wanamaker store, both below and above the street.

The clear glass base of 1234 Market East is not only a break with the two older buildings but a means of disclosing the real function of the street level of this office building: it is public space more than it is a lobby, designed to work integrally with the transportation mall concept, moving people in off-the-street spaces both vertically and horizontally.

1234 MARKET STREET EAST, Philadelphia, Pennsylvania. Owner/developer: *1234 Associates.* Architects: *Bower & Fradley, George M. Ewing Co.* Engineers: *George M. Ewing Co.* Lighting consultant: *Sylvan R. Shemitz & Associates.* General contractor: *Turner Construction Co.*

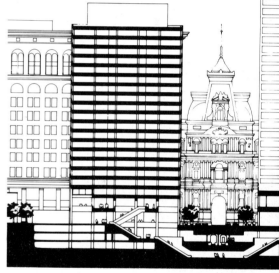

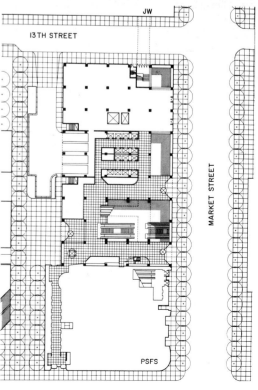

Rollin La France photos

3

The 8th and Market Street subway entrance is a *place* more than it is a building, but it nonetheless has an important architectural impact. It is seen in the course of a year by many Philadelphians, because it is the one point where all four of the main city lines can be reached: the main east-west (Market Street) subway is here attached to the main north-south line (Broad Street) by the Ridge Street connector, and there is another connector line for the high-speed New Jersey commuter trains. This new entrance replaces what was before just a stair leading down from the sidewalk, and it is the city's intention to line the concourse level with commercial shops, although neither these nor the structure intended for the adjacent street level vacant lot have been started yet. Mitchell/Giurgola also has proposed a continuous slide show of advertising that would be projected on the cement plaster wall of the glass-enclosed area at night, and the city has accepted this idea enthusiastically.

Facing the 8th and Market corner are three of Philadelphia's major department stores: Strawbridge and Clothier, Gimbel's and Lit Brothers—whose nineteenth-century building is seen at the center of the large photo, right. Its façade is a combination of cast iron and brick and details of these active, lacy façades are a contrasting foil for the simple forms of the Mitchell/Giurgola scheme, and are usually reproduced in the reflective surface of the glass. As can be seen in the section (top right, page 176), the upper glass panels lap over the panels below like huge shingles, so reflections are always fragmented. A large weathering-steel sculpture is being prepared for placing on the concourse level, among the patterned floor bricks, and it will complete this rejuvenation of an important subway stop in Philadelphia.

8TH AND MARKET STREET SUBWAY CONCOURSE, Philadelphia, Pennsylvania. Architects: *Mitchell/Giurgola Associates—James K. Wright, project architect.* Engineers: *Schulcz and Padlasky* (structural); *Vinokur-Pace Engineering* (mechanical). Contractor: *Lane Company.*

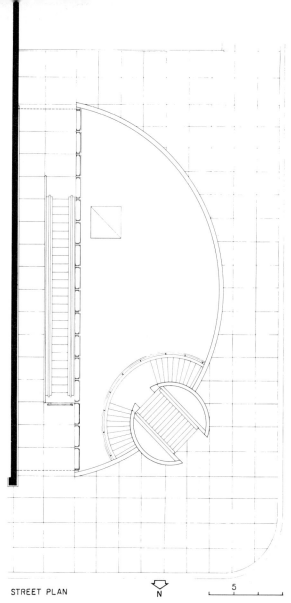

SECTION

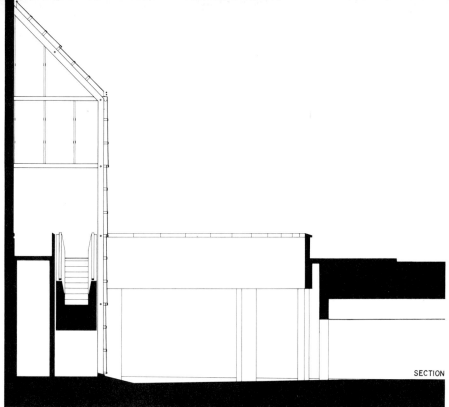

The subway stop is a simple
redevelopment of the street level
and the concourse level (plans,
right), with a protective glass
enclosure for the main escalator
between the two. There is a
generous stairway that has also become
an architectural event, with the
inside surface of the stairway
cylinder painted a bright yellow.
The escalator housing is open to
the outside at all times and
unheated, and the blank concrete
walls are beginning to carry the
ubiquitous and sometimes expressive
Philadelphia graffitti.

STREET PLAN   N   5

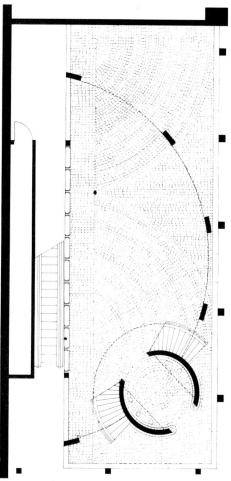

CONCOURSE PLAN

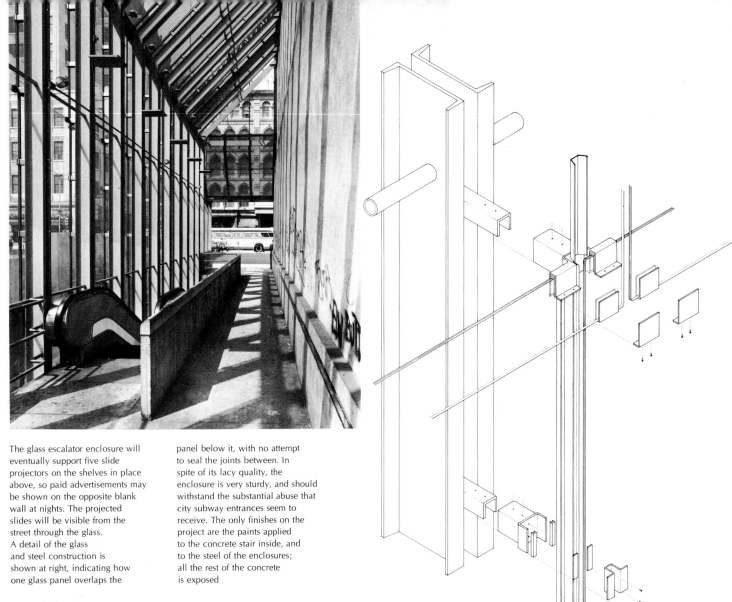

The glass escalator enclosure will eventually support five slide projectors on the shelves in place above, so paid advertisements may be shown on the opposite blank wall at nights. The projected slides will be visible from the street through the glass. A detail of the glass and steel construction is shown at right, indicating how one glass panel overlaps the panel below it, with no attempt to seal the joints between. In spite of its lacy quality, the enclosure is very sturdy, and should withstand the substantial abuse that city subway entrances seem to receive. The only finishes on the project are the paints applied to the concrete stair inside, and to the steel of the enclosures; all the rest of the concrete is exposed

4

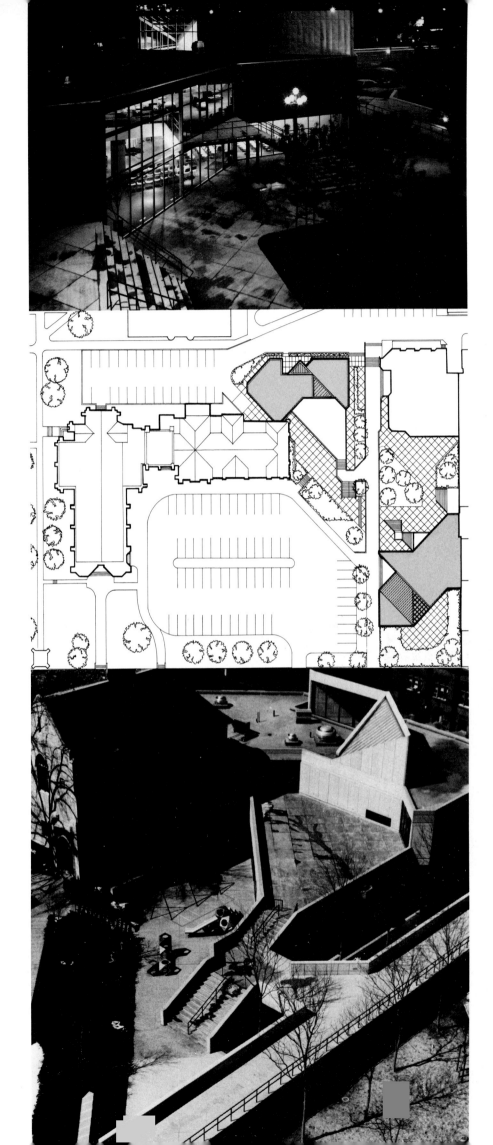

Six years ago, the University Circle Development Corporation initiated plans for a religious center on the Case Western Reserve University campus in Cleveland. The first buildings completed on the site were the Hillel Foundation, a Jewish center, and an addition, by Richard Fleischman Architects Inc., to the existing Church of the Covenant parish hall designed by Ralph Adams Cram. This new addition consists largely of educational space—rather open in plan—for youngsters engaged in an ongoing program of religious education. Standing in forceful contrast to Cram's neo-Gothic structure, the new addition is expressed in sharply faceted forms of concrete and glass.

When these centers were operational, the Bishop of Cleveland commissioned Fleischman's firm to extend the ecumenical concept by designing a Roman Catholic center across the plaza, eventually to be known as the Hallinan Center. Two flexible areas were required in Hallinan Center: a large hall where chaplain and students can meet to plan for worship, fellowship or related recreational activities and a small space to be used as a lounge and counselling area. The large photo on page 179 shows the architect's solution with the small space on the balcony overlooking the larger space below. In contrast to the Church addition, the exteriors employ very extensive glazing to create a transparent quality from the plaza that, hopefully, acts as an open invitation to potential users.

The connective tissue linking all the buildings is a multi-level plaza, free and playful in design, reflecting the diagonal geometry of the new buildings and expressing symbolically the ecumenical character of the complex.

ECUMENICAL CENTER, Cleveland, Ohio. Architects: *Richard Fleischman Architects Inc.* Engineers: *Gensert Peller Associates* (structural); *Andrew Psiakis* (mechanical); *Ralph Linton* (electrical). Landscape architects: *John Litten & Associates*.

Erol Akyavas photos

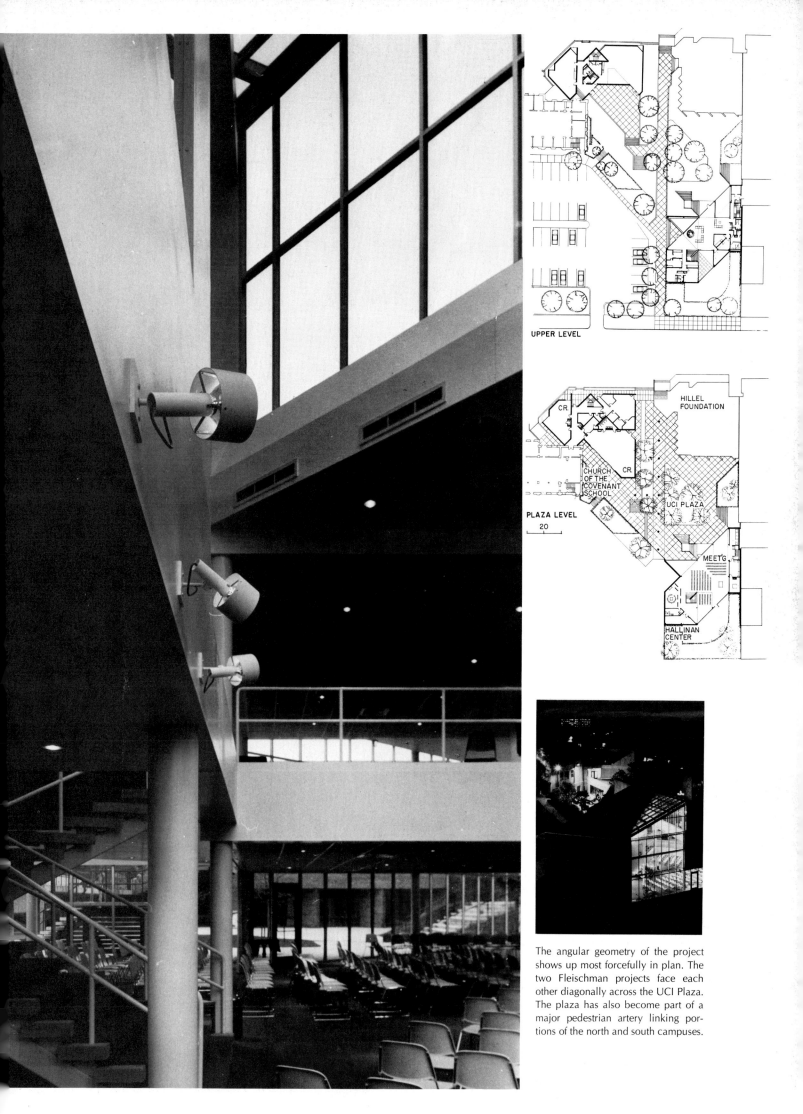

UPPER LEVEL

HILLEL FOUNDATION

CR.

CHURCH OF THE COVENANT SCHOOL

CR.

UCI PLAZA

PLAZA LEVEL

20

MEET'G

HALLINAN CENTER

The angular geometry of the project shows up most forcefully in plan. The two Fleischman projects face each other diagonally across the UCI Plaza. The plaza has also become part of a major pedestrian artery linking portions of the north and south campuses.

Philip Molten photos

5

Redevelopment in San Francisco's Western Addition gave the First Unitarian Church the opportunity to expand both its physical property and its program of activities within the community. The new buildings provide facilities where groups of various sizes, from 15 to 400, can meet, and these are made available for use by the community as well as by church members and organizations. There are also new church offices, a church school, an art room, a child care center, and a new chapel. The new structures are placed on the perimeter of the site, leaving a central atrium which is used, in good weather, as a social center. Daylight from the atrium floods a spacious gallery which surrounds it and which is both an exhibition area and the main circulation for the complex. The old church—built in 1889, and a survivor of the 1906 earthquake—and the new buildings achieve a remarkable harmony despite the difference in their styles and the periods they represent.

THE UNITARIAN CENTER, San Francisco, California. Architects: *Callister, Payne & Rosse*. Engineers: *Stefan Medwadowski* (structural); *O'Kelly & Schoenlank* (mechanical/electrical). Landscape architect: *John Carmack*. Contractor: *Pacific Coast Builders*.

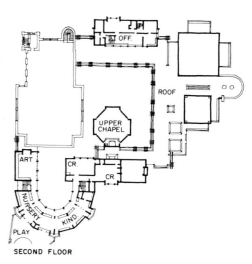

SECOND FLOOR

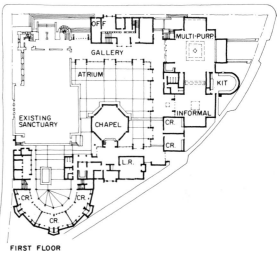

FIRST FLOOR

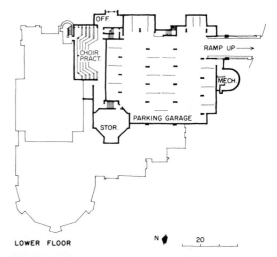

LOWER FLOOR

N 20

The handsome rough-form concrete stairs (above) lead to nursery and kindergarten. The chapel connects by the gallery (left) with the meeting rooms and is just a few yards from the old church. The multi-purpose room (below) and adjoining informal room are the main facilities for parish social activities. Under this area is a garage for 36 cars and a choir practice room which doubles as a small arena theater.

Philip Molten photos

6

The 51-61-71 project in downtown Vancouver, British Columbia, is part conservation, part new development. It includes preservation of the old courthouse and its formal plaza, with conversion of the building to civic/cultural uses, and construction of a new courthouse at the far end of the new three-block-long park which is to be developed on three blocks behind the old building.

Each of the three blocks of the park will have quite specific functions—51, for instance, will be essentially a civic-cultural complex; 61 will contain a low building with public roof gardens for the Provincial Government; the new Law Courts Building will be on 71—but the concept of the park as three-dimensional is the governing factor in the design. The buildings are important in themselves, but in the overall plan, they are elements, not dominants. It is the park that becomes the unifying means of relating old and new, open and closed space, high and low building levels.

The concept of the complex as a park directly reflects the stated wishes of Vancouver's citizens, who expressed their desire for a place for public gathering, for outdoor events such as art and craft shows, for ice skating in winter and sculpture shows in summer. They also wanted an art gallery and performing theaters. The "three-dimensional park" provides for all these, with the art gallery and the performing theaters in the converted old court house, and the sculpture court adjoining it. There are many open spaces for gatherings and for shows of various kinds. The Provincial Government Services Center is to be a low building designed as a series of roof gardens.

The most dramatic structure in the complex will be the new Law Courts Building, a terraced building with a sloping glass roof through which there are views to the North Shore Mountains. With careful regard for scale, the height of the new building has been kept to that of the old.

51-61-71 PROJECT, Vancouver, British Columbia. Architects: *Arthur Erickson Architects.* Engineers: *Bogue Babicki & Associates* (structural); *Reid Crowther & Partners, Ltd.* (mechanical); *W.T. Haggert & Co. Ltd.* (electrical); *Morgan A. R. Stewart & Co.* (engineers and surveyors). Consultants: *William Lam Associates Inc.* (lighting); *The Environmental Analysis Group* (programming). Director of design for Government of British Columbia: *Walter W. Ekins.* Construction manager: *Concordia Management Company Ltd.*

David Rizzoli photos

7

Natural landmarks, often important design elements in cities, present urgent design problems in scale and character for any new development nearby. When these problems are understood and sensitively handled, growth and change are acceptable events in urban life.

San Francisco's Telegraph Hill presents such a challenge. The residents of the Hill, deeply concerned with conserving those aspects of the area and its surroundings that make it precious to them, have successfully fought down a number of proposals which in their view would have materially altered both character and scale of the neighborhood.

But the problems of Telegraph Hill's scale and character are complex: on the Hill itself, below Coit Tower, are both single-family houses of varying size, and low-rise apartment buildings, so placed on the slopes that they seem integral with them. At the base of the Hill is the North Waterfront industrial area, with bulky warehouse buildings rising as high as 90 feet. Of recent years, the most sought-after sites for new development have been at the base of the Hill, where some sites have been razed and others hold only empty buildings.

The problem on new buildings is that Hill residents are little disposed to look down on and across new roofs of commercial or residential projects unless they are convinced that what they will see neither offends nor obstructs their outlook. As a consequence, the developers of Telegraph Landing, a residential complex of 600 units at the foot of the Hill, wanted a design which would be economical for them to build, satisfy the Hill residents, and need no variances from stringent height limits.

The solution by architects Bull Field Volkmann Stockwell—and their handling of conferences with neighborhood groups—met all three requirements, and produced what will be, on completion next year, a handsome, integral new part of the Hill community. Elevator penthouses were located in basements, and roof gardens were designed for rooftops of lower buildings to make the view from above as pleasant as possible, an effect enhanced by varied building forms and staggered heights.

TELEGRAPH LANDING, San Francisco, California. Architects: *Bull Field Volkmann Stockwell*. Engineers: *George S. Nolte & Associates* (civil); L.F. Robinson & Associates (structural); *Montgomery & Roberts* (mechanical). Landscape architects: *Royston Hanamoto Beck & Abey*. General contractor: *Cahill Construction Co.*

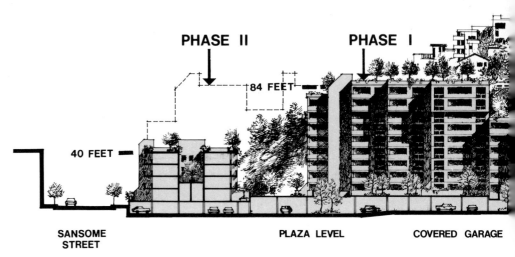

PHASE II   PHASE I

84 FEET

40 FEET

SANSOME STREET   PLAZA LEVEL   COVERED GARAGE

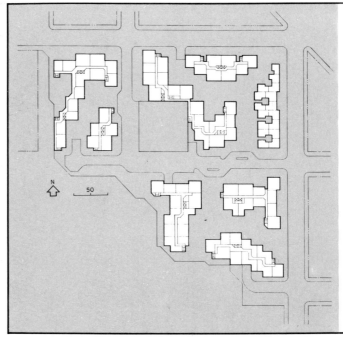

Telegraph Hill got its name from signals sent from its summit to announce the arrival of ships as they came through the Golden Gate. Departing ships often needed ballast which was provided by rocks quarried from the side of the hill. One of these quarries forms the backdrop for Telegraph Landing, the first phase of which is now under construction. The scale of the small houses and flats that now cover the hill, combined with the height limits set a few years ago, were strong design determinants—and constraints—which were resolved within the zoning envelope by the variation in building (and unit) types and heights, and in façade articulation and materials.

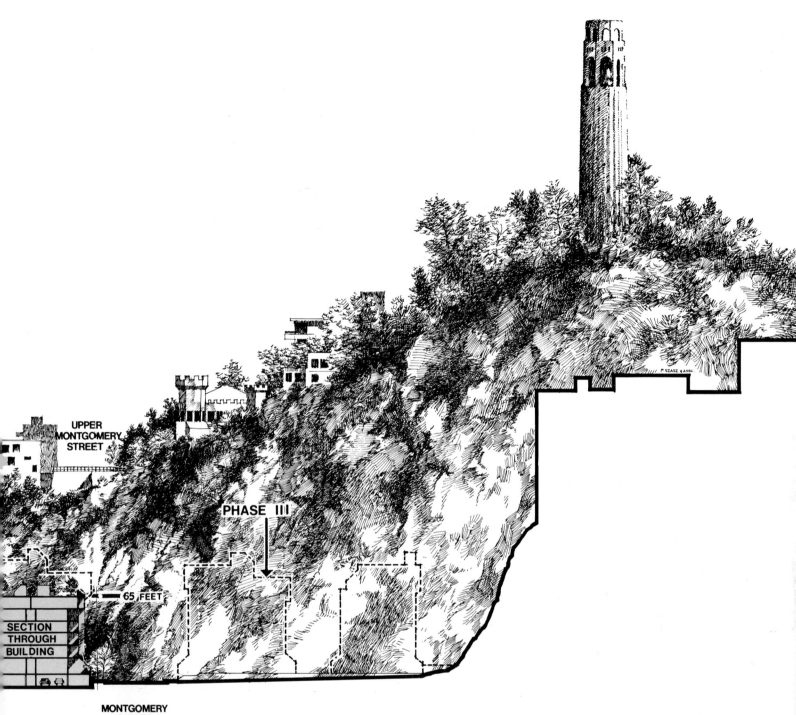

UPPER
MONTGOMERY
STREET

PHASE III

65 FEET

SECTION
THROUGH
BUILDING

MONTGOMERY
STREET

TOWNHOUSES

8

Any major new addition to older buildings requires that the architect be a bridge between one era and another; between an earlier time in a culture's history whose old forms remain intact, and the present time that almost certainly demands new forms to express new intentions. Usually, the architect today will not attempt any accurate reproduction of the old building.

The New York Bar Center by James Stewart Polshek is a case in point. Yet the enlightened architectural compromises shown here were not obviously necessary from the beginning; they had to be fought for to be achieved, and most other preservation projects will have to be, too. The New York Bar Association's first intentions when the headquarters was being considered four years ago, were to remove all four of the early 19th century row houses then on the site, and build an entirely new structure. Before the architects had barely finished first schematics on this part, several members of the Albany Historic Sites Commission got wind of things, and began publicly denouncing the project's intentions. Of course, it was not just that Albany might lose four fine row houses; the most important part was where the row houses were. As the aerial photo and site plan at the immediate right indicate, these houses form part of the boundary for one of Albany's finest small parks, one that eventually leads to the Capitol building itself, two blocks away. The stakes were the preservation of four individual buildings, the quality of the space in front of them, and ultimately, the still-intact 19th-century continuity of the whole district. Soon the Hudson River Valley Commission (a New York State agency) held a public hearing on the issue, and the result was

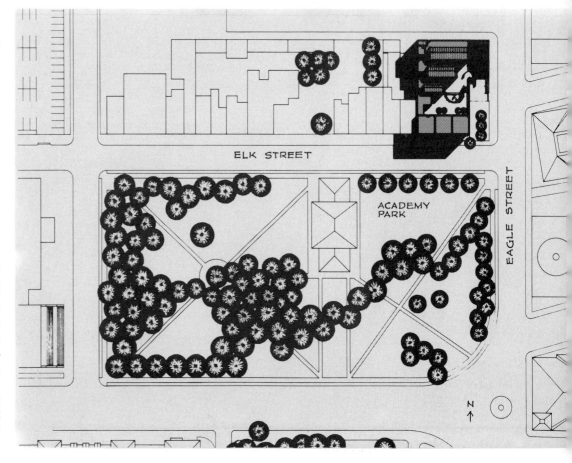

The preserved Elk Street façade of
the Albany Bar Center is shown
at the right, while the photo
below shows the major new addition
that has been connected at the
back. The aerial photo
at left shows the neighborhood context
of the new center, including the
continuing line of residential
façades of which it is a part, Academy
Park which these old houses face,
and several of the New York
State government buildings that also
face the park. Preservation of
this neighborhood context
was a major justification for saving
the three old houses as part of
the new Bar Center.

George Cserna photos

a judicial order barring any demolition whatsoever. All this (it must be emphasized because it is important) happened before either the architects or the owners had any substantial design commitments at all.

The architects insisted to the clients that the four row houses could be saved, although of course they said it would cost more money to save them, and it did. The Bar Association reconsidered the project. It came to see its own self-interest within a sufficiently large context, and almost any preservation project requires this kind of broader perspective if it is to be achieved in the face of direct economic calculations.

As these photos show, Polshek's final scheme uses the front half of three of the original four row houses, with the main entrance to the Bar Association now through house number one, shown in the middle photo, far right. The fourth row house (it used to be on the corner that is now grass and trees) was incorporated into the design too, but it developed severe structural cracks during construction. Consequently, the fourth house was removed entirely. Such unforeseen structural and construction problems can be related directly to placing new work in conjunction with existing, and these problems are usually typical.

Concrete caissons were used to shore up the old foundations of the houses, but soil conditions at the site were not ideal. Concrete driven into the ground of some Albany soil tends to cause uplifting in concrete that has been previously placed; "bulls liver" soil, it is ominously called. Consequently, most of the new construction is placed on grade beams and spread footings. Removing the house that failed structurally and restoring the old façades added $80,000 to the project's cost,

The new Bar Center has created a large
exterior court between old and new,
as the photo below shows.
The main entrance to the Center is
still through row house number
one (below, center) but a
major secondary entrance lies through
the court. The three principal
spaces of the new addition
have skylights, set within the
three peaked roofs of terne-
coated stainless steel.
These three loft-like spaces are spanned
with reinforced concrete beams,
resting on concrete bearing
walls and columns.

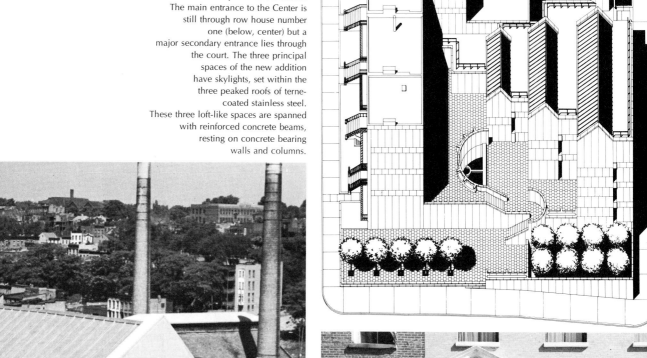

The perspective section at right shows the relationship of new and old spaces. the major interior is the Great Hall (below, right), which functions as a library, lounge, and social reception area for the Center. The space is 40 by 66 feet, and is filled dramatically by Norman Laliberté's bright banners, depicting various mottos, scenes and events from legal history. The interior below looks into the small reception and sitting room from the Great Hall, then out to the interior court.

and about $205,000 went into foundation problems caused by the poor soil. These foundation costs can be related in part to saving the old structures; it is rare that preservation of old work in conjunction with new will come out cheaper.

The exterior of the new work at the Bar Association is Indiana limestone, and that material has been carried across the Eagle Street wall of the existing row houses, as the photographs show. Except for this material connection, Polshek's new smaller scaled geometric forms are a contrast to the simple large rectangle that the old houses exhibit (perspective section opposite). The new work is larger in total volume than the old work saved, but it is fragmented into three simple pieces outside that cascade downward, descending and bowing toward the large single rectangle of houses. These three skylighted spaces recede in area in plan, too, as they near the older houses. Major interior spaces of the new work have been kept *underneath* the new courtyard and entrance level, thus using the slope of the site away from the houses in the rear to further reduce the exterior mass. It is this kind of architectural content that keeps the addition from overpowering the houses, while the new work itself remains clearly committed to the late 20th century in which it was built.

The function of the New York State Bar Association is that of providing information to its member attorneys across the state, disseminating information to the public, acting as a lobbying arm in the New York State legislature, and monitoring ethical standards within the profession. For these purposes, the new Center is the working base for about 40 men and women.

NEW YORK STATE BAR CENTER, Albany, New York. Architects: *James Stewart Polshek and Associates— James Stewart Polshek, project architect, Howard M. Kaplan, associate in charge.* Engineers: *Aaron Garfinkel Associates* (structural); *Benjamin and Zicherman* (mechanical). Landscape architects: *Johnson and Dee.* Graphic design: *Arnold Saks, Inc.* Banners: *Norman Laliberté.* Interior design: *Pamela Babey.* General contractor: *McManus, Longe, Brockwehl, Inc.*

LEGEND:
1. Storage and expansion
2. 1st Floor, reception
3. Maintenance staff
4. Hinman Library
5. Garage
6. Employee's lounge
7. The Great Hall
8. Reproduction and records
9. Mezzanine:
 Conference room
 Public Relations Department
 Accounting Department
10. 2nd Floor:
 Executive Director
 Foundation Office
 Continuing Legal Education
 Meetings and Membership
11. 3rd Floor:
 Grievance Hearing Room
 Counsel
 Staff Attorneys
 Legislation Offices
12. Courtyard

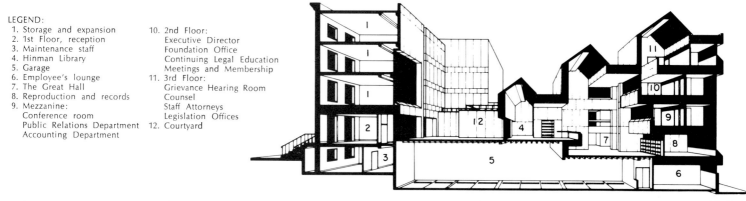

9

The Brooks Gallery has been a source of civic pride in Memphis since its dedication in 1916. Designed by James Gamble Rogers and modeled on the garden pavilion of the Villa Capriola, it has an irreplaceable grace, and a healthy scale for the surrounding area of large well-kept houses. When Mrs. Samuel Brooks donated the $100,000 construction cost in 1912, "art" was looked on as a rather elitist matter—but times change. The number of visitors and donors (including Samuel Kress) grew. In 1955 the building was expanded directly to the rear, but the addition was too small at the time of the dedication. At such a juncture, the solution has often been new construction of such overwhelming scale that preservation seems irrelevant. Architects Walk Jones and Francis Mah's housing for the new spaces, as seen at right, might well have produced that result. But . . .

Otto Baitz photos

Not all the planning of the new museum space involved massing problems. As the present design began, the expansion program was way behind schedule. There were the usual budget deficits that delays produce. Lacking was a set program on the nature of exhibits or the manner in which they were to be seen. Another serious problem was the fact that long-range expansion locations had never been considered despite on-going donations and steadily increasing public interest.

The shortness of schedule and budget were tackled by use of a prefabricated concrete construction system developed for low-cost housing (more on this later), but the scale of structural members had to be greatly increased. Large flexible areas were the only way to accommodate the indefinite exhibition program, and height was required for the appropriate spatial character. The operating economies of centralized facilities (versus the alternate of branch museums) produced an eventual 100,000-square-foot long-range expansion program—all on this site. This addition represents only a quarter of that area (see plan below), but plans for another increment are already under way.

The architects always intended that theirs would be a background building to both the original small-scale gallery and surrounding Overton Park. Given the volume of required space and the large-scale construction system, controlling visual impact was not easy.

There were two basic massing decisions made: the new first-floor level was depressed a full story below the original, and only half of the actual height is revealed from the front approach. The visual bulk is further broken into segments stepping back on a 45 degree sight-line from the older entrance façade. With such effort at sublimating its presence, it is remarkable that this background building can stand on its own design merits, as can be seen by moving around it (photo top right). The architects describe their façades as an abstraction of the Rogers exterior. The new concrete wall finish resembles the older limestone facing. Still the wall panelization and opening scale are as much a direct outcome of the construction method and interior considerations as they are deference to the earlier building.

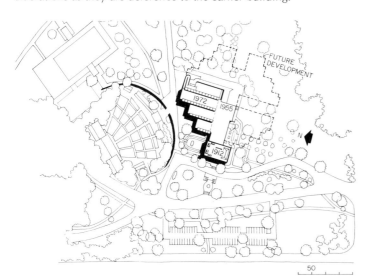

A ground slope was utilized to conceal the visible height from the front approach. The full extent of the new building is seen in stages. Passing around the original gallery the viewer first sees the most forward of three segments successively set back to reduce visual bulk (photo, top right). Farther around the new building, the slope begins to reveal the true massing (next pages, below), and finally the full height is seen from the rear (top left) where a berm conceals the sculpture court and a bridge spans between exit and stairs.

The addition is entered at a second part-floor seemingly suspended by separation from the walls. The other two views show the relation of the second floor to the first. A full orientation to the double height space is gained before descending the stairs. To accommodate the indefinite program, floor areas were kept as open as possible, but certain divisions were inevitable. Because of loading dock location, more temporary exhibits are housed on the first level, where direct access to trucks is available.

Francis Mah explains the firm's design concerns thus: Although the space was to be open, it was not to be amorphous, and the finished building shows strong visual direction. There are controlled views of the park outside, and the exterior sculpture court is related to the interior by the long horizontal glazing at the first level. A continuous circulation flow, without backtracking, and a visitor's understanding of location without signs, are successful planning results. Lighting was a primary concern, and the architects' preference was to maximize natural sources. The high skylights deflect direct sun to protect the exhibitions. In an open floor plan, an inherent lack of necessary wall space exists, and hanging plywood cubes were designed to be built locally at a third of the original display system budget. Museum director Jack Whitlock is highly pleased with the new building. He can now organize the artwork presently stored (by a weeding-out process of rotating exhibits), accept traveling shows, and bring professional as well as community-related programs to life. He now plans to carpet the first level which will weaken the visual contrast with the upper (carpeted) level, but allow a more comfortable relation between art and viewers.

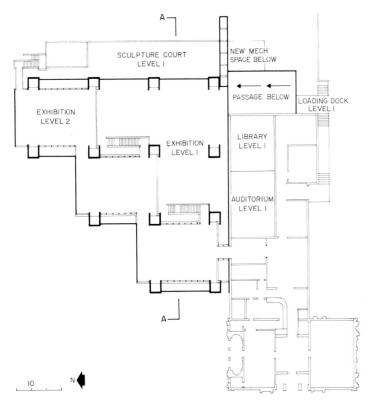

The Mah-Le Messurier Construction System used here was originally developed for the architects' local housing authority work, and possessed proven cost- and time-saving advantages for taller buildings. It relies on simple pre-cast concrete members made of U-shaped support cores, beams and double tees with concrete panel infill walls. The straightforward expression can be seen in the photos. The spans and, consequently, the scale of members had to be increased from previous applications. Manufacturing and handling of the new sizes (plus the lack of inherent system efficiency only gained by greater heights) produced structural costs in the neighborhood of standard poured concrete construction ($238,000), but the erection time was only eight weeks. The overall construction cost was held close to $30 per square foot (well under the original budget). This is particularly surprising when the special detailing is considered. The stair treads (photo, page 197) are individually cantilevered from the adjacent wall by tension-rod supports capped with the visible special fittings. Separations between the walls and second floor have railings of laminated glass to facilitate views to the floor below. The confines of the structural system were employed to produce spaces of great visual interest within the rectangular grid of massive-support cores. These carry mechanical risers, break up the otherwise open space, and provide a diagonal orientation to the course of travel.

THE BROOKS MEMORIAL ART GALLERY ADDITION, Memphis, Tennessee. Owner: *City of Memphis*. Architects: *Walk Jones & Francis Mah, Inc.—Francis Mah, principal-in-charge of design*. Engineers: *Le Messurier Associates, Inc.;* (structural): *Henry C. Donnelly;* (mechanical). General contractor: *Harmon Construction Company, Inc.*

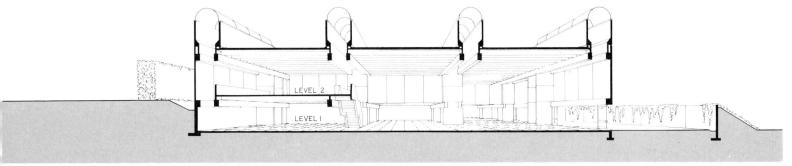

SECTION A-A

The townhouse is located among pre-1890-vintage houses in the historic district of Brooklyn Heights, and is one of three designed by the architects on the same block. Though differing in program requirements, all three (which can be seen in the photo to the left) were designed to relate closely to each other—and to the scale and texture of the houses existing on the street. Materials, fenestration and the over-all symmetry of the facades respect the formal rhythm of the older houses. But the house suits modern needs and attitudes as well, with modern materials, spaces, and design. Pink-toned concrete block and redwood trim were chosen to complement the city fabric, and are handled with the same sophistication as the very handsome, contemporary interiors.

Norman McGrath photos

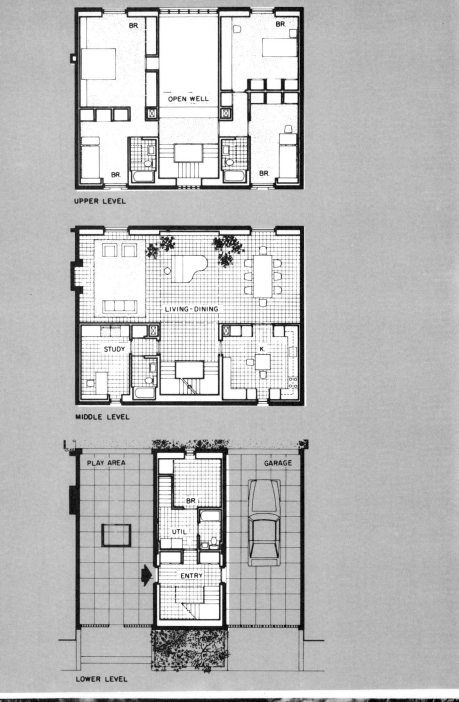

UPPER LEVEL

OPEN WELL

BR.

BR.

BR.

BR.

MIDDLE LEVEL

LIVING-DINING

STUDY

K.

LOWER LEVEL

PLAY AREA

GARAGE

BR.

UTIL.

ENTRY

10

This sophisticated city house for a four-member family was designed in the context of an established Brooklyn residential street. In addition to the general requirement of privacy, the owners requested an outdoor playground for their children—and ample space for formal entertaining for themselves. On-site parking, a study, studio-guest room and garden were other special requests.

The uncluttered design of both facade and plans reflects the architects' neat solution for these varied spatial needs. Order is the key to the efficiency—and livability—of a city house: in this design, great order has, paradoxically, brought great freedom and openness as well.

The living area is centered on the second floor, which is, except for the kitchen and a study-guest room, composed of a single space. A central double-height "core" of space cuts the floor above in two. This two-story area both zones parents' and children's bedroom wings and creates the great open quality of the design. The bedrooms are linked by an open third-level balcony, which exploits the visual potential of this room.

Space gained on the street level by raising living areas is devoted to a central entry, utilities, a covered play area and a garage. The play area extends outdoors into the private garden to the rear for an overall flow of space that is rare in private city living. The car—like children, often neglected in urban residential schemes—is integral to this design.

Windows and doors are organized for a trim, uncluttered look that reflects the trim, symmetrically ordered interiors, and, outside, lends great dignity to the pattern of the city street.

RESIDENCE FOR MR. AND MRS. LEONARD GARMENT, Brooklyn, New York. Architects: *Joseph and Mary L. Merz.* Engineers: *Paul Gugliotta* structural); *McGuiness & Duncan* (mechanical). Landscape architect: *A. E. Bye.* Interior design: *Ben Baldwin, Joseph Merz.*

11

Located amid the historic architecture of a quiet, tree-lined Georgetown street, this Washington, D.C. townhouse shows well that residential design can be contemporary and innovative, while respectful of an established neighborhood.

The architect's solution uses timeless materials in their natural state—burgundy-colored brick and gray slate—to keep the texture, scale and rhythm of the existing street. Materials combine with new interpretation of the traditional arch, bay window and mansard roof for a forceful design statement, in which the sculptured front bay windows especially are thoroughly modern in their expression of interior space.

Rooms were designed by the architect for a dramatic and uncluttered look usually found in a much larger house. Living room furnishings include silk and molded plastic or leather and chrome chairs. Floors are stained oak. Front rooms—the dining room and kitchen on the second floor and the master bedroom on the third—have a view of a park across the street. Back rooms—second-floor living room and other bedrooms —face a private garden. All are also oriented to two circular stair towers, which form the visual focal points of the house. Each stairwell includes view-through openings, and is capped with a 10-foot plastic dome to bring sunlight down through all the house. White walls and designed lighting add to the expansive quality of the scheme, which packs a great deal of comfort into an urban lot, thus offering its owners many qualities of a detached, suburban house with the many advantages of urban living.

The traditional townhouse, which fulfills a contemporary need, has, in this very spirited design, found a thoroughly contemporary expression.

RESIDENCE FOR MR. AND MRS. STEVEN TRENTMAN, Washington, D.C. Architect: *Hugh Newell Jacobsen.* Engineer: *James Madison Cutts.* Landscape architect: *Lester Collins.* Interiors: *Hugh Jacobsen.* Contractor: *The Brincefield Company.*

Behind their brick house, the owners can enjoy a secluded garden, equipped with fountain and slate floors on two levels and giving onto the living room via sliding aluminum doors. Kitchen and dining room are two steps up, a story above the entry. Special curved bricks were architect-designed.

Robert C. Lautman photos

12

An ingenious proposal to help solve the problems of family relocation caused by urban renewal demolition, the Boston Infill Program ("BIP" as it is called locally) seeks to use the countless parcels of existing empty land which are scattered over the city, and quickly build houses made of modular, precast components.

As the lots are of widely varying sizes, and in all sorts of neighborhoods, a quiet, flexible design with brick-veneer facades has been developed.

The program is conceived as one that can be executed on a crash basis: "only if a massive input of large, low-income family housing is available during the next 12 months will it be possible to avoid serious hardship for displaced families. To achieve this goal, it is proposed that planning, financing, community programing and site acquisition for 1,000 units of such housing be compressed into a 60-day period by total cooperation and maximum effort of all parties involved. Construction would be organized on a CPM system based upon initial occupancy within six months." The 1,000 units would be 30 per cent 3-bedroom, 50 per cent 4-bedroom, and 20 per cent 5-bedroom. From the financial point of view, it would be a "program of private, low-income, subsidized family housing."

The construction system incorporates a series of pre-cast, pre-stressed concrete wall, floor and roof panels which can be rapidly erected into modular concrete boxes with door and window units cast into the walls. The brick-veneer façade is designed to be pre-cast into the exterior walls.

Of standard depth, the units can vary in width by assembling a variable number of concrete components into each building. Stairs and mechanical systems are designed as individual packages to be quickly installed.

BOSTON INFILL PROPOSAL. Architect: *Stull Associates, Inc.* Engineers: *Sepp Firnkas Engineering* (consulting); *Engineering Design Associates—Peter S. Myers, president* (mechanical/electrical). Developer: *Development Corporation of America.*

Kimball / Rankin photos

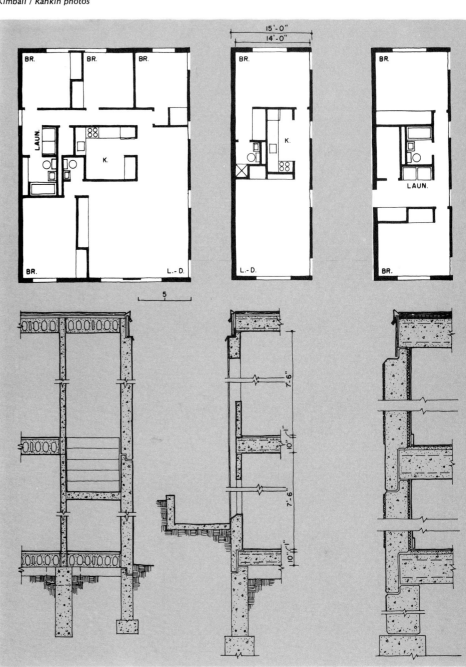

From the system of basic components shown in the diagram below, houses of a variety of plans and sizes can be speedily constructed to fill existing empty lots. A typical completed house is shown in the model photo above left. The photos above illustrate the step-by-step installation of the component units.

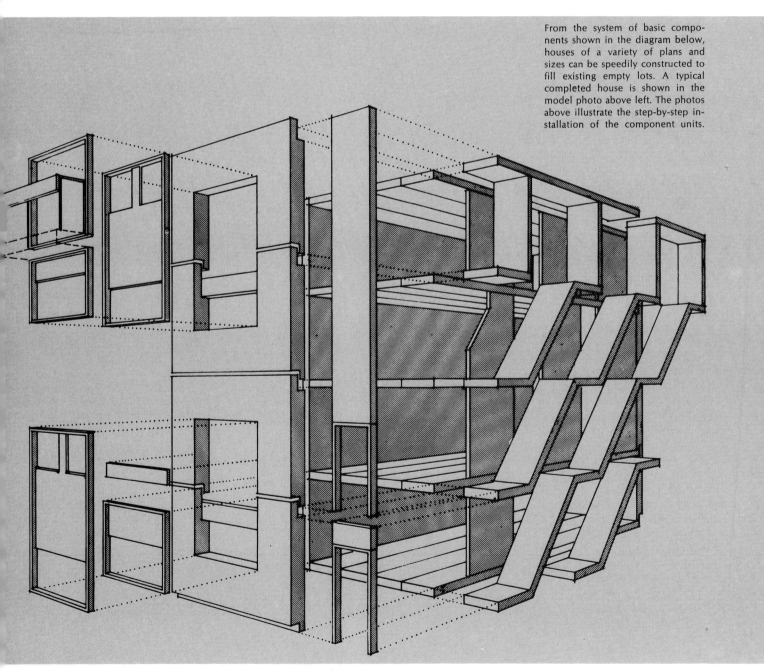

13

When the Home For Aged Men in Portland, Maine, was ready to expand, it could have torn down the fine old residence it was utilizing, and started over. The house was in adequate condition, but it violated many of the more stringent code requirements developed over the last ten years for this kind of housing, and needed to be completely "modernized." But it was not torn down; it was saved and used as the esthetic keystone for further development of the property, as the photograph at right so nicely shows. Now both the old home and the major new addition that it generated are housing elderly people, and maintaining the architectural continuity of the 18th-century residential neighborhood around them. And the people of Portland, Maine are publicly praising both the sponsor and their architect, as they should.

The old Levi Cutter House, built ca. 1810, with extensions added during the 19th century, was placed in trust by Mr. Cutter when he died to be converted to a home for elderly men. It remained in this use until 1964, housing from six to 24 men in a kind of boarding house arrangement. Then the board of directors of the trust decided they should try to enlarge the effectiveness of the home, and hired the young firm of Bruce Porter Arneill as their architects. Arneill studied the problem, and came up with the solution on these pages. As Arneill puts it: "The basic concept was to have the old and new buildings complement each other, and the space be-

The three plans below show the
major floors of the housing complex,
and the grading, with the previously
existing facilities overlaid
in grey. The long neck linking
the two parts allows a clear division
between the two, creates an adequate
space for an entrance vestibule
and allows the corridor to slope
up or down to meet existing
floor heights. The original house,
it is apparent, had several additions
to it between 1810 and 1900.

Bill Maris photos

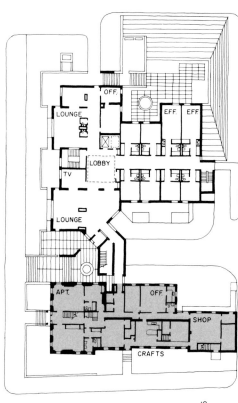

FIRST FLOOR

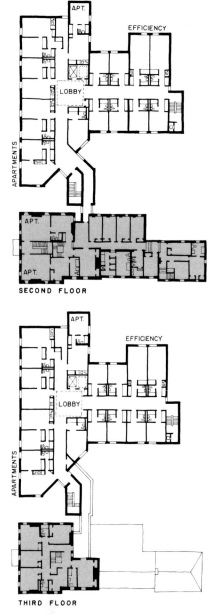

SECOND FLOOR

THIRD FLOOR

The west end of the new additio
(below) is designed so that the corrido
on each level can plug into a futur
addition, and the new elevatorin
and kitchen system has been designe
to accommodate this future additior
too. Below, the interior of th
new lounge looks onto the street, an
some of the other early 19th-centu
architecture of the neighborhood
At right, the new main entrance
the home fits between the old an
new buildings. The major horizont
elements of each façade line up
give unity to the who

tween invite you in. . . . We studied all the pertinent characteristics of the older building, and these influenced the detail design decisions on our new work."

The first problem of designing a compatible addition was one of scale: the finished new facility was to house 85 people, both men and women, rather than the six people it had housed for the last few years, so it would have been easy to dominate the old house with the new addition. The problem was solved by maintaining the roof line of the house, by making the windows in the new addition about the same size as the old window shapes (including the shutters) and by matching the old brick as closely as possible. The mansard roof of the addition allows a fourth floor to be worked in while still maintaining a three-floor roof line.

Matching the floor elevations in the old house was a problem, because new construction generally requires a greater floor-to-floor height than the nine feet of the original building. The nine-foot height was accomplished by using brick bearing wall construction, concrete planking for the floors, and by eliminating dropped and suspended ceilings except in certain corridors. The interior ceiling height is still maintained from eight feet to eight feet six inches throughout. The front façade of the new addition is in exactly the same plane as the façade of the house, and about three times as long, but the undercutting for terraces and porches that occurs at the ground floor of the addition lightens its mass effectively. Because the addition went up four stories, large parts of the site became avail-

able for terracing and exterior use (photo, top right) that would not have been available if an earlier two-story concept had been continued.

The old stairway of the original house is intact inside, as well as most of its original moldings. What the architect has added is paint; paint in bright colors and broad stripes to give the interior of the house a fresh new life without permanently harming any of its old forms. The house and its earlier additions now provide sleeping rooms for 22 people, plus activity and storage areas. The new addition houses the kitchen, dining room, administrative offices, lounges, and 15 one-bedroom apartments, eight efficiency apartments, and 27 single rooms.

The main entrance to both the old and the new parts of the complex is now between the two structures, shown in the large photo, opposite. The steps here are fewer than in the old entrance, and because of the grading of the site a person can avoid all steps into the building from the parking area at the rear.

The Park-Danforth Home has room sizes that are substantially larger than the FHA standards for elderly housing. There is no Federal money at all in the project; the original trust itself put up about half the funds and local Portland banks put up the other half. Total cost of the addition and rehabilitation together was $1,100,000.

PARK-DANFORTH HOME FOR THE ELDERLY, Portland, Maine. Architect: *Bruce Porter Arneill.* Engineers: *Rudolph Besier* (structural); *Francis Associates* (mechanical). Interior design: *Raymond Doernberg.* Contractor: *Consolidated Constructors & Builders, Inc.*

Index